Contents

KU-039-585

PART 4
Quality issues

Using Learning Technologies

This collection of first-hand accounts from experienced and accomplished learning technology practitioners highlights issues in using learning technologies for flexible, distance and open learning.

Drawing on their own experience, the authors identify and explore the most practical and complex issues faced and reflect upon the lessons learned. The definition of learning technologies is broad, encompassing not only the tools (print, audio, video, online applications) but their creative and informed application and social effects. Experiences from eight different countries are presented while the themes addressed include policy development, teaching skills, learner guidance, evaluation and reflective practice.

The stories recounted here speak directly to practitioners, researchers and administrators: they provide a model for reflection and offer practical guidelines for comparison with the reader's own experience.

Elizabeth J. Burge is a Professor in Adult Education at the University of New Brunswick, Canada. **Margaret Haughey** is a Professor in Educational Policy Studies at the University of Alberta, Canada.

RoutledgeFalmer Studies in Distance Education
Series Editors: Desmond Keegan and Alan Tait

Using Learning Technologies
International Perspectives on Practice

Edited by
Elizabeth J. Burge and Margaret Haughey

London and New York

First published 2001
by RoutledgeFalmer
11 New Fetter Lane, London EC4P 4EE

Simultaneously published in the USA and Canada
by RoutledgeFalmer
29 West 35th Street, New York, NY 10001

RoutledgeFalmer is an imprint of the Taylor & Francis Group

Typeset in Times by Steven Gardiner Ltd
Printed and bound in Great Britain by
Biddles Ltd, Guildford and King's Lynn

British Library Cataloguing in Publication Data
A catalogue record for this book is available from the British Library

Library of Congress Cataloging in Publication Data
Using learning technologies: international perspectives on practice /
Elizabeth J. Burge and Margaret Haughey, [editors]
　　p.　cm. – (Routledge/Falmer studies in distance education)
Includes bibliographical references and index.
1. Distance education – Computer-assisted instruction. 2. Educational
technology. I. Burge, Elizabeth J. II. Haughey, Margaret. III. Series.
LC5803.C65 U75 2001
371.3'5 – dc21　　2001019568

ISBN 0-415-21687-7 (hbk.)
ISBN 0-415-21688-5 (pbk.)

Contributors

Elizabeth J. (Liz) Burge began work in distance education in South Australia in 1978 followed by 20 years of varied activity in Canada including course design, evaluation, research, writing, and distance-mode teaching (her students comment that she asks "brain-burning" questions). Her doctoral research (Ontario Institute for Studies in Education, University of Toronto, 1993) examined adults' online learning experiences. Her practice so far, including leadership activity for the Canadian Association of Distance Education and work on international editorial boards, always leads to more nuanced questions. During 2000–01 she is Guest Professor, Flexible Learning, at Mitthögskolan in mid-Sweden, on leave from the University of New Brunswick in Atlantic Canada where she is a professor in adult education.

Catherine (Cathy) Cavanaugh is an associate professor in the Centre for Work and Community Studies at Athabasca University, Alberta, where she teaches women's studies and history. She has coedited three books on western Canadian history, published various refereed articles, and been awarded two prizes for an article about women's places in western Canadian history. Cathy's current research focuses on the biography of an Albertan female politician, the cultural uses of sex and gender in the social formation of western Canada, and the Prairie Women's Memory Project (to find, deposit, and document material related to women's history in western Canada).

Evelyn Ellerman is an assistant professor of communication studies at Athabasca University (AU), Alberta. For over 20 years Evelyn has taught communications and comparative literature with a focus on women and world literature, technology, and society. She heads the Communication Studies program at AU, a liberal arts program delivered entirely by distance. When wearing her comparatist hat, Evelyn writes about indigenous literatures of the Pacific Islands, in particular the life writing of women; currently she is writing a book on the literary decolonization of Papua New Guinea. When wearing her communications hat, Evelyn writes about the role of technology in education; she recently gave a keynote address at the Pacific History Conference in Canberra on the roles and responsibilities of the university in the digital age.

Charlotte N. (Lani) Gunawardena is an associate professor of distance education and instructional technology in the Organizational Learning and Instructional Technologies Program at the University of New Mexico, where she developed the graduate program in distance education. She has been active for the past decade in conducting research on distance education and has numerous publications and national and international presentations to her credit. Her recent research examines the design and evaluation of social-constructivist online learning environments, social presence theory, cultural factors influencing online group dynamics, and the evaluation of telecommunications-based distance education. She currently serves as a principal investigator and evaluator for a five-year, US Department of Education-funded Star Schools math and science project. Lani is originally from Sri Lanka and consulted on a World Bank-funded teacher education project there in 1999. She enjoys international consulting and travel.

Claudia Harvey is the UNESCO Representative (Northern Caribbean) and Education Advisor for the Caribbean. A citizen of Trinidad and Tobago, she has over 20 years of experience functioning at middle and senior executive management levels, including being a former director of the University of the West Indies Distance Education Center and a former permanent secretary in her native country. She has conducted social and educational policy research and provided consultancy support in management and change in the social sectors (education, health, community development and gender, and development). She has 30 years of experience in teaching and/or curriculum development and evaluation in primary, secondary, tertiary, and nonformal education. She earned her doctorate in higher education at the Ontario Institute for Studies in Education, University of Toronto.

Margaret Haughey, a professor in educational policy studies at the University of Alberta, has been involved in distance education for over 30 years. At various times she has worked as producer, director, writer, researcher, designer, and presenter with schools and universities in the development of their distance education programs and presently coordinates the development of online graduate courses in her department. She enjoys the eclectic nature of such work. In her other academic life she focuses on policy and practice related to educational administration and leadership and supervises doctoral student research. Her research and writing have been equally wide-ranging, from the understandings of learners to administrative and policy issues in schooling and tertiary education in both distance and conventional education. As Editor of the *Journal of Distance Education*, her current interests are in flexible learning.

Judith Kamau is one of southern Africa's foremost teachers, researchers, and practitioners of distance education, particularly in the areas of instructional and course design, course writing, the production of learning materials, and pedagogical theory and practice for distance education. Since 1995 she has been a senior lecturer and Head of the Distance Education Unit, University of Botswana, responsible for the administration, management, development, and implementation of distance education programs. Judith also works extensively with other educational institutions in the southern African region and has organized and led numerous workshops and tutorials. She is a consultant for various international organizations and a widely published author. Her coauthored *Guide in Designing and Writing Distance Education Materials* for UNESCO should be published in 2001. Judith holds an MA (London) and a postgraduate diploma in mass communications (Nairobi). Fluent in reading and writing braille, she developed braille correspondence courses for blind students at the Hadley School for the Blind in Nairobi, Kenya, where she was Assistant Director 1977–81.

Erin Keough has been associated with the fields of distance education and telemedicine for over 20 years and since 1995 has been the Executive Director of the Open Learning and Information Network (OLIN) in Newfoundland, Atlantic Canada. OLIN is a provincial coordinating agency mandated to facilitate partnerships among public and private agencies involved in distance learning and telehealth in the areas of new media development, electronic networking, and international partnerships. Erin has considerable international experience and has directed projects in the Philippines, Japan, the Caribbean, and Kenya. She has served in a variety of capacities on many boards such as the Canadian Network for the Advancement of Research, Industry and Education (CANARIE), the National Advisory Network of Experts for the Office of Learning Technologies (Human Resources Development Canada), and the Canadian Association of Distance Education (CADE) of which she was President.

Gill Kirkup is a senior lecturer in educational technology in the Institute for Educational Technology (IET) at the Open University, UK, for which she has worked for over 20 years. Extended employment in one institution not only has enabled her to develop and diversify her activities and expertise, but has also provided the opportunity to integrate them across discipline boundaries. Gill has published extensively on aspects of gender and technology and gender and distance education. She divides her time between these activities, institutional research on the use of ICTs in teaching, and developing her own online teaching and course development skills.

Christine Marrett has been involved with the evolution of distance education at the University of the West Indies (UWI) since 1982 when she managed an experimental project using interactive audio-teleconferencing for the delivery of distance education programs in the three-campus, multi-country setting of the UWI. She is now Campus Coordinator and Senior Projects Officer of the UWI Distance Education Centre on the Mona campus, Jamaica. Her qualifications include a master's degree in public sector management from the UWI and a diploma in the practice of higher education, which she completed as a distance education student of the University of Surrey in the UK.

Edith Mhehe is a tutor and senior faculty member at the Open University of Tanzania (OUT). She has worked for more than 15 years as a curriculum developer at the Institute of Education, Dar es Salaam, Tanzania, where she designed and evaluated geography study materials for secondary schools, coauthored and published geography course books and teacher guides, and conducted nationwide inservice secondary school teacher training. She joined the Open University of Tanzania as founding Dean of the Faculty of Education in 1994 and is now undertaking doctoral studies at the University of Alberta, Canada. Her research examines the difficulties faced by Tanzanian women who are considering or participating in higher education through the OUT and how the university can enhance the participation of women.

Lori Oddson is the Director of Collaboration and Learning Services at Athabasca University (AU), Alberta, Canada. She began work at AU in 1978 as a part-time chemistry tutor. Ten years later she moved into a full-time administrative position to play a key role in the delivery of on-site courses at various collaborating institutions in the province, several of which involved partnerships with First Nations communities. Now that AU has extended its mandate to include all of Canada and the rest of the world, and the number and type of partnerships has increased dramatically, Lori is involved in negotiating agreements and identifying suitable delivery modes and instructional methods. Her commitment to distance education has much to do with her belief that adult learners require flexibility and choice.

Lucille Pacey bases her consulting practice on over 18 years of experience as a senior executive in distance education. As Vice-President of the Open Learning Agency in British Columbia, she had direct operating responsibility for the Open University, Open College, Open School, and the Knowledge Network. She has set up corporate policy and overall strategic direction for the effective use of technology and telecommunications for the delivery of education for school-aged children, adults in postsecondary education and professional training, and for the general public. Her interests span the public and private agenda for the encouragement and development of an economically viable multimedia industry in Canada. She is the North American Representative of the World Education Market scheduled for a second meeting in 2001. She has served as President of the Canadian Association for Distance Education.

Christine von Prümmer is a sociologist with more than 25 years of experience in educational research and evaluation. She joined the German Fern-Universität (Distance University) in 1978 and has worked in the areas of course evaluation and institutional research, addressing issues such as the situation of women and men in distance education, communication patterns in distance education, and the use of information and communication technologies in distance education. Throughout she has focused on gender issues and, with Gill Kirkup of the UK Open University, has conducted and published comparative empirical research. Her doctoral study on the role of distance education in the social mobility of women drew on data from her evaluation research and resulted in the book *Frauen im Fernstudium. Bildungsaufstieg für Töchter aus Arbeiterfamilien* (Campus Verlag, 1997). Her second book *Women and Distance Education. Challenges and Opportunities* has been published in the *Routledge Studies in Distance Education* series.

Judith M. (Judy) Roberts has over 25 years of experience in national and international applications of learning technologies, with particular emphasis on distance and open learning and telemedicine. Before starting her consulting practice, Judy Roberts & Associates/Associés Inc., she worked from 1974–90 as senior founding staff member of projects such as Telemedicine in Newfoundland and Labrador, Telemedicine for Ontario in Toronto, and Contact North/Contact Nord in Sudbury, Ontario, Canada. She is an adjunct faculty member of the Graduate School of Management and Technology, University of Maryland University College, Consulting Editor to the *International Review of Research in Open and Distance Learning* published by Athabasca University, Alberta, and a member of the Office of Learning Technologies (Human Resources Development Canada) Advisory Network of Experts. She is editor of the French- and English-language series *Lifelong Learning on the Information Highway®/ L'apprentissage à vie sur l'inforoute (MD)* (1998, 1999) and coeditor of *Why the Information Highway? Lessons from Open and Distance Education* (1995) (www.robertsassoc.on.ca).

Ute Rossié is a social scientist with 20 years of experience in evaluating distance education at the German FernUniversität, where she has worked and published mainly on the situation of women and men in distance education, communication patterns in distance education, surveys of graduates, study goals and motivation, and, increasingly, the use of information and communication technologies in distance education. Together with Christine von Prümmer she has set up a research program that focuses on gender issues and questions the underrepresentation of women in university-level distance education in Germany. In addition to ongoing evaluation projects (among others access and use of ICTs, the careers of graduates, students' interest in international distance education courses, students in Eastern Europe) she is currently involved in developing and testing research instruments for online evaluation.

Suzanne Sexty is the Library Instruction Coordinator at Queen Elizabeth II Library, Memorial University of Newfoundland Atlantic. She considers herself fortunate to have been able to spend her career in the same profession, most at QE II. Her work has involved roles from book page to head of technical services, and her responsibilities have ranged from rare books to library instruction. These positions have given her numerous opportunities to use and develop different sets of skills and have fueled her lifelong interest in learning and teaching styles. Although her present responsibilities are primarily for students taking courses on campus, she has expanded *campus* to include distance education learners. In the 1957 movie *Desk Set* Spencer Tracy compliments Katherine Hepburn on her office and asks her if she likes working there. More often than not Suzanne would echo her reply, "If I didn't work here, I'd pay to get in!"

Barbara Spronk is the Director of the International Extension College (IEC) in Cambridge, UK. Before coming to IEC in 1997 she spent more than two decades at Athabasca University (AU), Alberta, where she held a variety of posts ranging from course author and tutor to Director of Regional and Student Services and International Liaison Officer. For most of her time at AU she wrote, tutored, and coordinated courses in anthropology and women's studies. She holds a doctorate in anthropology from the University of Alberta. She has managed development projects in Thailand and Canada and worked as a consultant and trainer in more than a dozen countries including Guyana, Ghana, Sudan, Namibia, Bangladesh, and China. As part of her work at AU and IEC, she has written two books and a dozen articles and made innumerable presentations at conferences and other gatherings. Despite continual travel she is currently engaged in a number of writing projects.

Mary Thorpe began work in distance education in 1972 as a mass media tutor at the then University of Botswana, Lesotho, and Swaziland. She joined the UK Open University in 1975, researching tuition, counseling, and the regional support system for students. She has contributed as author and educational technologist to courses in Third World studies, adult learning, open and distance learning, and communication technology. Her publications other than course materials have emphasized pedagogies appropriate to adult learning and flexible and lifelong learning. She has also developed and evaluated approaches to fostering reflection in distance education courses. Her *Evaluating Open and Distance Learning* brought these themes together in a handbook for practitioners that has been widely used. Since January 1995 Mary has been the Director of the Institute of

Educational Technology (IET) at the UK Open University. IET has an international reputation for its research in and development of technology in the service of student learning. She was appointed to a personal Chair in Educational Technology in 2000.

Lantana Usman is a lecturer in education at Amadu Bello University in northern Nigeria. She has been Head of the Social Studies Unit, which offers teacher preparation courses both on site and through distance education. She has been involved in research on issues related to school dropout and rehabilitation of the boy child from Quranic education (UNICEF), health care and nutrition concerns for nomadic women, commercial exploitation of the girl child, and sex education workers and AIDS education in the suburbs of northern Nigerian towns. She holds an M.Ed and an M.B.A., and her publications range from the issues of the textile industry to financing of primary education. Her doctoral research examines the implementation of the government's Nomadic Education policy, and in particular the expectations, implementation, and outcomes of their programs for women and girls.

Arlene Young is an associate professor of women's studies at Athabasca University, Alberta, with over 25 years of experience as a counselor, manager, and teacher in distance education. As well as supervising the delivery of several undergraduate women's studies courses, she is developing a women's counseling program and teaches a gender issues course via the Internet. Arlene also has more than 30 years of experience as a community activist and advocate for social change with an interest in promoting woman- and child-friendly communities. Her doctoral research is on women's experiences of involuntary job loss.

Part 1
Introduction

1 Using learning technologies: An introduction

Margaret Haughey

What are learning technologies? As Ursula Franklin (1999) pointed out, technologies are not simply tools to be used in achieving a goal. They are systems that guide our actions; we may not recognize it, but technologies shape us while we shape them. A definition of technology as mere hardware and software is increasingly inaccurate – and not only for previous media such as print, radio, and television. It is even more limiting when discussing the latest digital technologies involving multiobject repositories, virtual rooms, and hypermedia environments. My understanding of technology has been shaped by the writings of McLuhan, Innes, Grant, and Franklin (Goyder 1997). They considered it to be the creative application of the known to achieve different goals or resolve particular problems. For them "technology includes the notion of tool use, associated techniques, use of knowledge and materials, and social effects" (Haughey 2000a: 122). In terms of learning technologies, Liz Burge and I used this broad notion of technologies to guide our work with this book.

Why learning technologies? Governments and business organizations have discovered alternative education formats (distance education, open learning, flexible learning) and seem, at least in the developed world, to consider them a part of the economic engine essential for a knowledge society in a global marketplace (Evans and Nation 2000; Haughey 2000b). As educators, we are faced with questions about the use and promotion of learning technologies involving supposedly flexible systems that do not support the learner or provide the learner with choice. We worry about the expanding gap between those who can access technologies and those who cannot and the pressure both to cooperate and compete with traditional classroom-based learning. We are confused by the desire to provide anytime learning that returns teachers to the sweatshop of a 24 hours/7 days per week response. Today, when the tension of responding appropriately to these issues is almost overwhelming, the advice of seasoned practitioners can help reground our practice and reaffirm the values we espouse.

I believe that in reexamining our use of learning technologies it is no longer sufficient to focus on practice; we also have to be cognizant of the policy initiatives and political realities that surround and sometimes threaten to overwhelm us. We need to know how to assess them in relation to our own understandings of the place of distance education and how to position our own ventures in relation to them. It is also, an opportunity to look again at our own understandings of policy development and implementation models and strategies. In addition, pressures for quality and accountability in education provide a further imperative to assess our work. Evaluation has its benefits: in providing information to enhance our understanding of what we are doing; in helping to guide future initiatives; and in directing the improvement of programs to which we are already committed, but where, without an understanding of the larger context, we are at a loss to assess the uses of this information. At the heart of our uncertainty is the desire to know how best to use learning technologies to promote access to learning that is relational, dialogic, informative, and timely. Liz and I therefore conceptualized using learning technologies as having three foci: policy issues, practice issues, and quality issues, and these form the major sections of this book.

Why reflections on practice? Despite Jennifer Moon's contention that current writing on reflection includes such "a chaotic catalogue of meanings" (1999: 3) that it is difficult to identify what it entails, reflecting on our practice has long been promoted in adult education as a way to better understand ourselves and the challenges we face. I do not see knowledge as separate and arising from experience through reflection, but rather that experience and knowledge are dynamically interactive (Johnston and Usher 1996). I support Usher's description of experience as embodied knowledge constructed in the doing, and reflection as giving voice to this personal knowledge that increases our self-awareness of our situation (Usher *et al.* 1997). Taken out of context, descriptions of practice can seem naïve or even simplistic, perhaps because practice itself is complex, contingent, dynamic, and problematic. Liz and I did not fully realize how difficult it is to recollect practice in context until we asked the authors to write descriptions of their practices; to comment on what they had learned; to tell how this new knowledge had changed their understanding of their own work – and then tried to do the same. We found that it is not easy to write about our practices, because what we do can seldom be captured adequately by a job description or even a diary of a day. So much is left out, taken for granted, passed over, forgotten, until someone asks, "But why?" or "Suppose?" and we are called back to the scene – or more accurately to its reconstruction – often unprepared for the emotions and feelings that were present then. As we worked with the authors, sharing drafts and discussions, seeking clarity and illumination, we appreciated their willingness to rethink, review, and rewrite, to be reflective practitioners.

Learning for me requires that social response. It includes not only the information I am able to obtain through listening and reading, but also involves explaining my ideas to others who share my interests and hearing their comments about my narrative. It is learning in the experience. As Dewey (1933) suggests, we may do much of our thinking alone; but it is in the discussion with others that we hear what we really think and see others' reactions. We surprise ourselves – "Did I say that!" we say with a mixture of laughter and awe – for our intuition sometimes leads our thoughts. Liz calls this process "talking to think."

For me insights often come through images embedded in stories. One such was in an article (Yamamoto 2000) where a teacher wrote of his desire to be considered a paddler rather than a rower. Rowers always faced backward, whereas it was the future that held excitement and promise for him. I thought about how the rower faces away from the goal, has to assume that there is less need for adjustment, and checks the course only occasionally with periodic glances over the shoulder. The paddler, in contrast, is focused on what is ahead, constantly correcting and guiding the canoe and making judgments to help reach the goal. The paddler seems to focus on the currents around the canoe, whereas the rower focuses on the rowing. I saw how we can be so caught up in our own work that other ways of seeing what is going on are lost to us. Like the rower, we focus on the rowing more often than the goal. I explored the merits of looking backward or forward. Reflection seems much like rowing; often the process seems focused on what has already occurred and on enhancing the means to a goal rather than examining the taken-for-granted context and choosing new strategies that seem to be the concern of the paddler. We sought to have authors examine both assumptions and strategies in their reflections.

How useful are their reflections to you? We asked practitioners from various parts of the world to document their experience in using various learning technologies, to situate that experience within a reflective practice orientation, and to propose context-sensitive guidelines for using learning technologies. We hoped that this would enable readers to legitimize their own experience and learn from peers in other contexts and that it would promote cross-cultural and multidisciplinary perspectives concerning the use of learning technologies. At the same time, we would like you to take away an enhanced sense of respect for learners and a reconfirmed valuing of the importance of their concerns. We desire for you a deeper understanding of the complexity surrounding the use of learning technologies, greater ability to respond to the tensions surrounding adoption of systems that are not learner- and learning-oriented, and better skills to challenge and critique the political and policy directions of the ownership, use, and implementation of learning technologies. We hope you will come away with an enhanced passion for relevance, whether it is in learner design, policy processes, or evaluation strategies. Liz writes more cogently and persuasively of our "vital guidelines" in the last chapter.

Our thanks to the writers who worked with us throughout the project: their stories of practice are the core of this book. We also relied on the contributions of many others and wish to recognize their assistance. We acknowledge the tangible assistance from the Commonwealth of Learning, which supported our vision of a book that would aid educators everywhere through sharing stories of experience, stories that help us learn from each other and draw us together in a community of practice. Now let me introduce the writers who will guide your learnings.

Outline of the book

Policy issues

The first four writers focus on policy issues and their implementation. Chapters on issues in the developing world (Spronk) and policy formation (Roberts, Keough, and Pacey) are followed by two on policy implementation in specific institutions (Marrett and Harvey, and Kamau).

Chapter 2 Barbara Spronk, who has traveled extensively in developing countries as part of her work, introduces fundamental issues related to learning technologies faced by women in the developing world and provides both statistics and vignettes to heighten our awareness. She delineates the impact of poverty on human choice and its influence on concerns such as the length of life, housing, health, water, and personal security. The prevalence of illiteracy and the lack of access to technologies are enumerated. She identifies four issues concerning technologies: access, control, costs, and choices. Access is often limited both in numbers and through male privilege and when available is usually expensive to maintain. Community centers, a common development choice, often depend on foreign donations or government support and on women having the money, time, and freedom to come to them. Lack of family support, whether overt (denial of permission to attend) or covert (requiring additional duties that ensure the person remains at home), is common. Even where women are able to participate, they are often not involved in decisions that affect their learning.

Chapter 3 Judy Roberts, Erin Keough, and Lucille Pacey focus on the importance of understanding and using government and institutional policy in support of distance education and flexible learning. They point out the need for educators to be aware of the policy process, to monitor it, to know how to get involved, and to be clear about the outcomes they are seeking for distance education. They use two Canadian cases to illustrate the key areas involved at government and institutional levels. Goals of government policy involvement were decentralized decision-making, linking education and economic development, enhancing access to new learning technologies, and maximizing the operational efficiencies of provider organizations. Policy areas at the institutional level involved the organizational structure and processes, the mandate, resource provision, stakeholder consultation, and technology partnering. They identify policy lessons learned and end with a list of recommendations about the need to be policy-informed, to analyze "key policy drivers," to understand the structures and roles of stakeholder groups, and to become involved early in the policy process.

Chapter 4 Policy implementation is often a major impetus for developing distance learning. Christine Marrett and Claudia Harvey provide a longitudinal look (1978–2000) at the problems and creativity of the University of the West Indies (UWI) in implementing distance education in response to government and stakeholder demands. They outline the steps adopted and the challenges they are still working through and provide a set of recommendations. Over the period, they describe the use of various technologies and the move from being a pilot project, an experiment, to being an enterprise. But although the distance education pilots were successful and distance education was recognized as an integral part of UWI, their success created other problems concerning the add-on nature of the distance education enterprise and the tension for faculty between on- and off-campus instruction. Some were policy issues concerning decentralization and the need for greater coordination, whereas others concerned students' attitudes to distance education and the scarcity of qualified tutors. The problem of upgrading technology remained ubiquitous. Communication and collaboration with partners are seen as essential strategies to address these challenges.

Chapter 5 Although major issues in policy implementation exist at the institutional level, policy issues for the department are concerned with the development of the distance learning materials. Judith Kamau describes the constraints on course development, on the selection and use of appropriate learning technologies, and on learner support in her experience in Kenya and Botswana. She outlines the course development model in use at the University of Botswana and identifies the strains on such a model from political announcements, lack of lead time and inadequate integration of the unit, and the dual-model institution. The shortage of qualified instructional designers and problems associated with borrowing courses from sister institutions are other issues. The intermittent level of access and lack of a solid technological infrastructure limits technology choices to print and audiocassettes. Face-to-face tutorial sessions are welcomed by students, but depend on the quality and training of the tutor for their success. She stresses the importance of regular monitoring to ensure quality throughout the system.

Practice issues

Judith Kamau's chapter, with its focus on course design, provides a link to this section on issues of practice. Cathy Cavanaugh and her colleagues speak from their own experience as teachers and student support facilitators about their ambivalence concerning of the influence of electronic communications technologies. Gill Kirkup uses her puzzlement about the person in the photograph on the class Web site to explore issues of identity, gender, and adult education. Suzanne Sexty examines the issues surrounding the development of a library Web site, and Lantana Usman critiques the provision of radio programs for nomadic Nigerian women and recommends their involvement at the program policy level. Edith Mhehe also addresses issues of policy in her chapter. Concerned at the lack of women registrants at the Open University of Tanzania, she illustrates how policy and practice converge in frustrating the women's opportunities to study and recommends institutional strategies for alleviating their concerns.

Chapter 6   Cathy Cavanaugh, Evelyn Ellerman, Lori Oddson, and Arlene Young are colleagues at Athabasca University, Alberta. They believe that relationships and personal interactions are integral to learning and teaching and discuss lessons they have learned "from the cyberclassroom," in particular, the pushes and pulls associated with the adoption of new learning technologies. They explore the gap between promise and experience for themselves. Their concerns include misgivings about becoming facilitators rather than teachers and of being overwhelmed by e-mails. But they also recognize that technologies can provide advantages to students from linking them together in conferences to being thought-provoking in a way that allows the person time to think before responding. They have chosen to add technologies carefully, examining the advantages and disadvantages of each addition to themselves and their students. They worry about the embeddedness of hierarchy and the limits of a dialogical process for students, so that although they accept the democratizing potential, they are "hyper-aware" of the influences of new technologies on the teaching–learning environment.

Chapter 7   Gill Kirkup picks up on these themes and addresses assumptions about situatedness, identity, authenticity, and embodiment in the online environment. Moving from recollections about the embodied experiences of summer residential schools at the Open University, United Kingdom (OUUK), she uses the provision of a photograph on an online course to question her own online identity as the teacher. Kirkup wonders if her identity is dependent on students knowing what she looks like, on knowing her gender, and how their conceptions of her affect their learning and her relationship with them. There is a taken-for-grantedness that the posted photo and biography are genuine, but they may not be of that person, and does truth matter here? Besides authenticity, identity is tied to authority. Kirkup questions whether we will be more likely not to post a picture, to post another's picture, or to feel that the photo we post betrays us if we do not think that the photograph matches the group's conception of an acceptable group member or a competent instructor. And then there is the question of which photograph matches one's own conception of all one's identities. An identity of responsiveness developed through student interaction in an online setting can tyrannize other personal identities if the demand for immediacy of response time is left unchecked. Kirkup calls for more research on the development of identities in online learning communities and on how as educators we can help people connect these to their embodied keyboarding selves.

Chapter 8   As Suzanne Sexty explains, the provision of library support services is often a difficult issue in distance education. Sexty, a university librarian, describes her challenges in designing an interactive Web site to provide research assistance and teach information literacy. She worked with librarians at other Canadian universities in the region to develop a site that all could access. In the process, she worked not only to develop the necessary skills to put up a Web page with hypertext, but also to ensure that there would be sufficient users to make her work and the time invested worthwhile. The three-dimensional nature of an interactive Web site and the need to design creatively for the low-end user were early challenges. The content required agreement among a wide range of partners from librarians to instructors in various disciplines. She used as her referent point the interactivity of the reference interview in face-to-face situations and so sought multiple entry points, a design that encouraged active participation, various learning options, and links throughout. She promoted assignment requirements that involved library research skills with instructors, and once the site was operational, developed a business plan to ensure its continued viability.

Chapter 9 Whereas Suzanne Sexty examines the use of the Internet to provide one kind of educational programming, Lantana Usman explores the possibilities and constraints on the use of radio programs for adult learning. She begins with a review of the involvement of nomadic women in the educational radio programs designed for the Fulani of northern Nigeria. Usman identifies the importance of the radio as a communication device for these women, but also highlights that the women are dependent on their men for access to the radio. Similarly, although the radio has been identified as an important medium for enhancing literacy, life, and entrepreneurial skills among the women, their programs are likely to be broadcast at inappropriate times, to be too didactic and monotonous, and to provide feedback that is at best sporadic. She suggests that in terms of policy development, the women's organizations should be consulted regularly; that more attention should be given to the women's lifestyles in the broadcast scheduling; and that the pedagogy and content should be changed to be more interactive, responsive, and culturally appropriate.

Chapter 10 Edith Mhehe examines the reasons for the low rate of participation of women in the Open University of Tanzania (OUT). She describes the results of interviewing over 80 women: students, former students, and nonstudents. Three barriers affected women's participation: lack of time and resources, cultural expectations, and financial issues. Given their other responsibilities, women students lacked sufficient time to focus on their studies. The delays in obtaining study materials exacerbated this difficulty. The female cultural norm is to attend first to the needs of the family and male relatives, and usually the woman's religious position and traditional expectations require the permission of her husband or male relatives to leave the home or to spend money. Women interviewees identified unique-to-women difficulties that were not acknowledged by the OUT system. There were issues of permission from husbands and from workplace supervisors and of safety and unpredictability in travel and accommodation arrangements. In terms of financial issues, the women identified the combination of high fees and low wages that made it impossible for many to access OUT and the hidden costs of travel and accommodation that were further limitations. Mhehe suggests that reviewing the present instructional system, providing more self-contained materials, ensuring the provision of bursaries or fee-release, increasing gender-sensitive staff development, and involving more women in the administration of the OUT are immediate steps that could aid women's participation.

Quality issues

The three chapters in this section are concerned with the evaluation of the design and implementation of courses and programs to provide information for policy-making. Gunawardena's work is driven by her research interest in online evaluation and her own experience with teaching online. Thorpe reviews issues of evaluation that have arisen in her experience with one institution, and von Prümmer and Rossié, who are also institutional researchers, focus on the evaluative questions that need to be asked to raise awareness of gender issues.

Chapter 11   Charlotte Gunawardena is a researcher who has focused on the development of methodologies and tools for evaluating online learning. In this chapter, she reflects on that decade of work at the University of New Mexico, the aspects that engaged her, and the discoveries that she made. Her first focus was on participation, and she used interactional analysis to diagram the linkages among participants in a peer support network of medical students. The particular model she used was able to identify numbers of interactions, but lacked a way to analyze the messages themselves. She found that adding content analysis helped, but realized that she needed to hear from participants about their interaction and to review students' unsolicited comments online. She used surveys to identify the variables that can predict students' satisfaction in online learning networks. Her results suggested that although there were three predictors, social presence alone was the strongest predictor. She then used a grounded theory approach to explore these predictors. Gunawardena is now exploring how learners experience being online. She has used analysis of conferencing transcripts to explore how knowledge is constructed in online situations. The metaphor of the patchwork quilt has been helpful to her in developing a model of the process of shared knowledge construction.

Chapter 12   Mary Thorpe reviews the current state of evaluation in relation to learning technologies. Based on her experience as an evaluator and as director of an institutional evaluation unit at the Open University (OUUK), she identifies the key issues facing evaluators as access and learner profiling, usability, the changing roles of learners and tutors, and new opportunities created by learning technologies. Access and learner profiling raise questions about who the learners are and whether and how they access the course materials as intended. Thorpe stresses the importance of piloting materials and especially the evaluation of the overall media mix and program design. Because new technologies bring changes in roles, it is important for evaluators to be sensitive to these changes and their potential impacts. The ease of Web-based course adaptation makes surveys of students' satisfaction with the course materials a routine occurrence. It also provides possibilities in that material from previous courses can be used as a resource for the current offering of the course. Strategies for gathering data have also changed. It is easier to reach students, and responses can be designed to be sent electronically and privately. Online interviews and the full course transcript are other means to gather qualitative data effectively.

Chapter 13   Christine von Prümmer and Ute Rossié are institutional evaluators at the German Distance University (FeU) whose work includes examination of issues related to women's participation in distance education. They undertake institutional studies and critique findings to ensure that gender bias or gender blindness is revealed and addressed. Von Prümmer and Rossié document a list of gender-related concerns for feminist researchers. These include the proportion of male and female registrants, gender-specific enrollment patterns and course choices, differences in learning styles, gendered learning contexts, and gender differences related to use of electronic communications technologies. They note that in relation to electronic communications technologies, researchers have found gender differences related to the types of applications used, online group problem-solving strategies, participation in discussion groups, navigating the Web, and preferences in Web design. Using their own work as examples, they illustrate the importance of looking beneath the survey responses to further questions about gender differences. In each instance, they point out the importance of linking these findings to institutional commitments that might reduce or eliminate these differences. Finally, they contend that gender-sensitive research is crucial, because without it the natural development of virtual universities is likely to replicate the gender biases present in traditional forms of distance learning.

Chapter 14   In the last chapter, Liz Burge draws from her own experience and her readings of the previous chapters to provide a reflection on the major themes in the book and a set of suggested guidelines for practice.

References

Dewey, J. (1933) *How We Think. A Restatement of the Relation of Reflective Thinking to the Educative Process* (2nd edn). New York: Heath.

Evans, T. and Nation, D. (2000) *Changing University Teaching. Reflections on Creating Educational Technologies*. London: Kogan Page.

Franklin, U. (1999) *The Real World of Technology* (rev. edn). Toronto: Anansi.

Goyder, J. (1997) *Technology + Society. A Canadian Perspective*. Peterborough: Broadview.

Haughey, M. (2000a) "New Information Technologies and Learning," in W. Hunter (ed.) *A Pan-Canadian Education Research Agenda*. Ottawa: Canadian Society for the Study of Education.

Haughey, M. (2000b) "A Global Society Needs Flexible Learning," in V. Jakupec and J. Garrick (eds) *Flexible Learning, Human Resource and Organizational Development*. London: Routledge.

Johnston, R. and Usher, R. (1996) "Adult Learning and Critical Practices: Towards a Re-theorization of Experience," *International Conference for Experiential Learning, South Africa, Abstracts*. Online. Available: http://www.uct.ac.za/depts/adult-ed/1996abst.htm (November 16, 2000).

Moon, J. (1999) *Reflection in Learning and Professional Development. Theory and Practice*. London: Kogan Page.

Usher, R., Bryant, I., and Johnston, R. (1997) *Adult Education and the Postmodern Challenge. Learning Beyond the Limits*. London: Routledge.

Yamamoto, K. (2000) "The Life of the Mind. A Tribute to Three Professors," *Change*, 33, 5, 48–50.

Part 2

Policy issues

Here we group the authors whose work describes policy development and policy implementation issues related to learning technologies. Barbara Spronk provides a contextual description of the sociocultural, economic, and political issues affecting learners in the developing world. Judy Roberts, Erin Keough, and Lucille Pacey outline the reasons for understanding the intricacies of policy contexts that operate in promoting and implementing learning technology networks. Christine Marrett and Claudia Harvey describe the institutional changes and challenges that were faced by the University of the West Indies as it worked through various stages of implementing distance education. Finally, Judith Kamau retrospectively analyzes the issues confronted by the University of Botswana and its progress toward establishing a distance education unit.

2 Naming the learning technology issues in developing countries

Barbara Spronk

The context

My task for this chapter is to name the issues that arise for women in the developing world in and around the uses of technologies for learning. This is a difficult task, perhaps impossible, given the complex, diverse, and multi-layered realities of women's lives. Consider, for example, the frustrations of the professional woman in, say, Sudan, who is unable to access her e-mail on the family computer because her son has changed the password without telling her. Her frustrations cannot easily be compared along any dimension with those of the woman who is living in one of the many communities of people in and around Khartoum who have been displaced from their home-lands by the war in the south. This woman's frustrations center on another kind of technology failure. She has managed to do everything she needs to do to get to her weekly tutorial for the primary health course she is taking. She has arranged care for her small children, cooked the midday meal for her husband, and carefully saved all week from the pay she earns as a worker in the local clinic to make sure she has enough money for the bus fares. And now the bus she is on, for which she has already paid her precious coins, has broken down, which means she will miss the other two buses she must take in order to reach the study center. No one set of issues, no one voice, can readily represent these divergent realities.

What we can do is to give voice to a multiplicity of realities that are grounded in women's experience in countries throughout the developing world. This book is doing this by having women from countries and regions in both the developed and developing worlds recount and reflect on both the joys and the frustrations of their experiences with technologies for learning. My voice is that of a worker in overseas education for development with extensive Canadian and international academic experience in distance education.

The particular locus of my work is a nongovernmental organization called the International Extension College (IEC, www.iec.ac.uk). Since 1971 the college has worked in partnership with agencies, organizations, and institutions around the world to improve the quality of life for people in developing countries through expanding their educational opportunities. The approaches we use in this work are primarily those of open and distance learning. Because of this focus, we continually face issues about the use of communications technologies and the media they make available for learning. We acknowledge that these technologies offer exciting possibilities for helping to conquer the barriers of distance both physical and social, to erase geographical boundaries, and to bring learners and teachers together in global classrooms.

Our excitement at the prospects that these technologies offer us is tempered, however, by the circumstances of those with whom we work. For the most part, these are organizations that work on the side of peoples who exist on the margins of the world's societies and polities. These peoples are marginalized in a number of ways. First, they live in the world's less developed countries, and many of them – 1.2 billion people according to the United Nations Development Programme (UNDP 2000) – subsist on incomes of less than a dollar a day. Second, in their countries and regions they are politically, although not always numerically, in the minority: for example, as refugees and displaced peoples; nomadic groups; oppressed ethnic, racial, or religious groups; out-of-school youth; unemployed and underemployed workers; or in communities far away from anything that could be called a metropolis. Third, if they are women in any of these groups, they are even further marginalized in terms of access to and control over the resources they need in order to sustain their lives and those of their children, whom they nurture as part of the work of sustaining their communities and ensuring their future.

At IEC we work at some remove from the direct realities experienced by these women at the margins. We cannot speak of the realities as those who live them can. Nonetheless, we continually face the danger of making easy assumptions based on our experiences of life and learning in the industrial world. So, for example, in delivering a workshop on integrating media in open and distance learning, we might schedule a session for discussion of online or networked learning. We always preface these sessions with the explanation that although this particular audience might not yet be in a position to implement Internet-based learning because of the lack of infrastructure and resources, this mode of learning offers exciting possibilities and may be available to them in the not-too-distant future. We also provide as many examples as we can of how the Internet is being used in contexts not unlike theirs. The response to this message is invariably mixed. A few Internet aficionados are usually among the participants, but mostly there is resistance even to the suggestion that at some point in the near future the Internet might be a feature of their delivery systems. To people who struggle to find enough money to keep the rent paid on their crumbling learning centers, or to ensure a regular enough supply of light bulbs so that learners are not literally in the dark, regular routine use of the Internet by teachers and learners sounds like science fiction.

The context of this resistance is poverty in all its various dimensions. Poverty deprives people of basic capabilities and renders our easy assumptions not just fictional, but potentially dangerous. In the section that follows a number of dimensions of poverty and their implications for marginalized women as learners are explored. Following this, the third section explores some of the particular issues raised for women in and around the use of learning technologies.

Poverty and women in the developing world

The focus in this chapter on marginalized women of the developing world should not be taken to signify that it is only those women that matter. Rather, as DAWN (Developing Alternatives with Women for a New Era, www.dawn.org.fj), a network of activists, policy-makers, and researchers from the economic South, proposes, "it is from the vantage point of the most oppressed – women who are disenfranchised by class, race and nationality – that the complexities of subordination can be best grasped and strategies devised for a more equitable development" (Kabeer 1994: 81).

As I indicated above, the lives of these women are constrained by poverty. The UNDP report analyzes human poverty trends in terms of what it calls "deprivation in basic capabilities" (UNDP 1997). This deprivation encompasses years of life, health, housing, knowledge, participation, personal security, and environment. As the report points out, "When these different kinds of deprivation interact, they severely constrain human choices" (UNDP 1997: 25). These factors constrain women particularly from access to the kinds of learning technologies that are available and appropriate for their use, as is argued below.

Years of life

A short life span is perhaps the most extreme kind of deprivation, and it is the dimension of deprivation with which the UNDP report begins. In developing countries nearly a fifth of the population is not expected to live to the age of 40, four times the proportion in industrial countries. In all those countries designated *developing* by the UNDP, female life expectancy at birth in the year 1998 was 66.4 years and in the least developed countries 52.9 years, compared with an average of 79.6 years for the developed (OECD) countries. Life expectancy is actually marginally higher for women than for men in the developing world; men's life expectancy at birth in 1998 was 63.2 years for all developing countries and 51.2 years for the least developed countries (UNDP 2000). At the same time, however, maternal mortality is acknowledged as a major contributor to high mortality in developing countries. In the developing world the maternal mortality rate in 1994 was 471 per 100,000 live births, more than fifteen times the rate in industrial countries (UNDP 1997).

Health

Life expectancy is closely linked to the provision of health services, adequate nutrition, and safe water. According to the UNDP, "The health backlog in the developing world is enormous. Nearly 800 million people lack access to health services ... and nearly 1.2 billion people lack access to safe water" (1997: 29). These particular figures are not broken down by gender. Indeed, as noted above, women appear to live slightly longer than men, even in the developing world. We have an indicator of gender disparities in terms of access to health services, however, in Sen's (1990) remarkable but substantiated claim that "More Than 100 Million Women Are Missing." Sen arrives at this number of "missing" women by comparing the number of women who are alive in the world today with the number one would expect to be alive given the ratio of human female to male births, which in industrial countries is typically around 1.05 or 1.06. In south Asia, west Asia, and China the ratio of women to men can be as low as 0.94 or even lower. In seeking an explanation, Sen examines "the complex ways in which economic, social, and cultural factors can influence the regional differences" (1997: 61) and finds that in developing regions where women have employment outside the home, own land and other property, and have higher education levels, the ratio of men to women approaches that of the industrial countries. These differences in women's economic independence and power, he suggests, "may have far-reaching effects on the divisions of benefits and chores within the family and can greatly influence what are implicitly accepted as women's 'entitlements,'" (1990: 63) including the entitlement to food and medical care. I return to this issue later.

Housing and environment

Housing is fundamental to the formation of human lives and capabilities and for the maintenance of communities. Yet according to the UNDP, more than a billion people in developing countries live without adequate shelter or in unacceptable housing. At least 600 million people live in dwellings that threaten their health and lives. An estimated 100 million people are without homes of any kind (UNDP 2000). Poor housing is often linked to poor sanitation, which in turn exposes people to infection and health risks. Approximately 40 percent of people in the developing world have access to proper sanitation, leaving more than 2.5 billion people with no access. Because throughout the world the burden of maintaining the home falls almost exclusively on women, the billion who are inadequately housed include at least half a billion women and girls who have to shoulder this burden under grim conditions. In addition, ongoing environmental deterioration is a source of continued impoverishment. For example, in sub-Saharan Africa 65 million hectares of productive land have become desert in the past 50 years. Salinization damages 25 percent of the irrigated land in central Asia and 20 percent in Pakistan. In developing countries a third to a half of urban solid wastes go uncollected, with serious health implications. And some environmental degradation – polluted air, greenhouse gases – migrates across borders, affecting poorer countries and people. For example, Bangladesh could see its already vulnerable land mass shrink another 17 percent with a 1 meter rise in sea level from global warming (UNDP 1997).

Personal security

The above dimensions clearly threaten the security of one's life as a marginalized woman. As the UNDP report puts it, "One of the less quantifiable aspects of deprivation, but one felt strongly in most poor communities, is a lack of personal security" (1997: 31). Most victims of crime and violence are poor. In addition, external and internal conflicts pose a considerable threat to personal security. There were 36 major conflicts in 1998. An estimated 5 million people died in intrastate conflicts in the 1990s. Globally in 1998 there were more than 10 million refugees and 5 million internally displaced people. The number of deaths and displacements alone greatly understates the human rights violations in these conflicts, which include widespread rape and torture (UNDP 2000). In the domestic sphere the worst threats of violence are those against women. It is estimated that about one in every three women has experienced violence in an intimate relationship, and that each year about 1.2 million women and girls under 18 are trafficked for prostitution (UNDP 2000).

Knowledge

At the most basic level of the knowledge and knowledge-related skills that are needed for what we casually term "modern" life, the developing world has more than 840 million adults who can neither read nor write. Of these (aged 15 and over), 538 million are women (UNDP 1997). In 1998 the female illiteracy rate was about 35 percent in developing countries and close to 60 percent in the least developed countries (UNDP 2000). The inability to read or write obviously bars women from the most basic tool in the distance educator's tool kit, the printed page. It also prohibits the use of the current object of attention – bordering on obsession – in the distance education world, namely, the computer and its related computer-based and computer-mediated learning applications.

In terms of such technologies for learning, developing countries have about 200 radios per 1,000 people, a fifth of the ratio in developed countries, and 140 television sets per 1,000 people, a little more than a fourth of the number in industrial countries. As for the electricity needed to power these machines, an indication of the gap between the industrial and developing worlds is electricity consumption in kilowatt-hours per capita. In industrial countries this rate in 1994 was 7,514, compared with 763 for all developing countries and 74 for the least-developed countries (UNDP 1997). The industrial countries' ratio of 350 main telephone lines per 1,000 people is more than four times the ratio in developing countries. Two statements that have been made in so many contexts they have become maxims are that there are more telephone lines in either Manhattan or Tokyo alone than in all of sub-Saharan Africa, and that more than half the people in the world have never made a telephone call.

Of particular interest in this Internet-obsessed age are some rather sobering, recently compiled statistics that compare rates of ownership and access in industrial countries with those in the developing world. The authors of the recently published *Vital Signs*, the Worldwatch Institute's gazetteer of world trends, claim that about 147 million people are wired to the Internet, almost half of them in the United States. Whereas one in four Australians is now wired, in Africa the ratio is one to 4,000 (*Guardian Weekly* June 6, 1999: 7). According to an even more recent estimate, this one by the US Commerce Department, 80 million Americans are now online, a number that will grow to 130 million in just over three years: half the nation's population (*Guardian Weekly* July 1–7, 1999: 33). The UNDP report, which focuses on globaliz-ation, recounts the results of national Internet surveys in 1998 and 1999 and finds that "within each region it is only the tip of each society that has stepped into the global loop, just 2 percent of all people," and that "current access to the Internet runs along the fault lines of national societies, dividing education from illiterate, men from women, rich from poor, young from old, urban from rural" (1999: 62). As for the numbers of women using this technology, they account for 38 percent of users in the US, 25 percent in Brazil, 17 percent in Japan and South Africa, 16 percent in Russia, 7 percent in China, and 4 percent in the Arab States.

Participation

The above figures suggest that in both industrial and developing countries, women are not participating in the world of the Internet to the same extent as are men. Given the general state of women's access to power and economic benefits, this is perhaps not surprising. In terms of the public sphere of life, in the words of the UNDP report, "Political space has always been monopolized by men" (UNDP 1997). In industrial countries in 1990 the number of female administrators and managers constituted 44 percent of the number of their male counterparts, whereas the equivalent figure for the developing world was 12 percent. For professional and technical workers, the figures were 95 percent for industrial countries and 64 percent for developing countries. For economic participation, the economic activity rate for women is about 70 percent of the rate for men in developing countries (UNDP 1997). (*Economic participation* is defined as supplying labor for the production of economic goods and services, including all production and processing of primary products whether for the market, for barter, or for one's own consumption.) As for women in government, the total participation rate for women at the end of February 2000 in the OECD countries was only 15.5 percent, only marginally higher than that in the developing world: 13.6 percent (UNDP 2000).

In the domestic sphere, turning once again to Sen, there is in the extensive literature on women and development considerable evidence that *"gainful* employment, i.e., working outside the home for a wage or in such 'productive' occupations as farming, as opposed to unpaid and unhonored housework, can substantially enhance the deal that women get" (Sen 1990: 63; examples of this literature include Mies 1982; Oppong 1983; Mbilinyi 1984; Benería and Roldan 1987; Sen and Grown 1987). Such gainful employment supplies women with an income that they can utilize more easily than they can their husband's income.

Employment can also confer enhanced status in the family and influence cultural traditions regarding who receives what benefits. When combined with legal protection, gainful employment can make women's economic position much less vulnerable. Finally, in Sen's words, "Working outside the home also provides experience of the outside world, and this can be socially important in improving women's position within the family" (1990: 63). Sen does not claim that gainful employment is the only factor that affects women's chances of survival. Education and economic rights, including property rights, "may be crucial variables as well" (1999: 64), in Sen's careful phrasing.

Naming the issues of technologies

Access, control, costs, and choices

In naming the issues that arise for women in the developing world in and around the uses of technologies for learning, I abandon Sen's caution and state simply that the issues facing women are fundamentally those of access and control, which in turn give rise to issues of costs and choices. Because women even more than men lack control over the strategic resources they need to sustain their lives, they are relatively disadvantaged in every dimension one can name.

These four issues apply to many women everywhere, not just those in the developing world. As pointed out in the above section, however, those women who are triply marginalized – by living in regions or countries termed *developing*, by their membership in those regions of marginalized groups, and in those groups by virtue of being women – particularly lack control because their lives are so severely constrained by poverty in its various dimensions. They are more likely to be ill and underfed, lacking in disposable income, property, and political influence, and unable to read or write. They are also likely to bear the burden of the socially vital responsibility of maintaining households and families under conditions of poor or nonexistent housing, sanitation, and potable water.

It is these constraints that render suspect any easy assumptions we might harbor about the benefits of learning technologies for marginalized women. It is unrealistic to expect that such women will own their own radios, for example. Even if there is a radio in the household, there is no guarantee that the women will have ready access to it as it is often the men of the household who control what is heard and when. Kenyan researcher Mary Ngechu, for example, runs a radio listening group scheme for female farmers. When she discovered that many of the women who came to the group meetings had been unable to listen to the program that week because their husbands had the radio tuned to something else (often football!), she reorganized the meeting schedule so that women could gather while the program was being broadcast and listen to it together (personal communication). Still on the issue of radio, the households where these women live are not likely to have reliable supplies of electricity, and batteries are expensive. Solar-powered and wind-up radios are available alternatives, but they are still expensive. As for the latest radio technology – offering quality audio via digitized signals – the cost of receivers puts the benefits of this technology out of reach of all but the richest families.

There are, of course, other avenues for making technologies available to women. Creating community "telecenters" is one approach. In the words of the 1999 UNDP report, "from Peru to Kazakhstan, basic telecenters have been set up in post offices, community centers, libraries, video shops, police stations and health clinics, providing local community access to telephone and fax services, email and the World Wide Web" (1999: 65). Women do use these facilities. According to research carried out in a community-based telecenter in a rural setting in South Africa, some 70 percent of the customers using any facility and 60 percent of those using the telephone were women. The women's main interest was the telephone, however, which they used when they had the money and were near the center to call friends and relatives, in particular their migrant-laborer husbands. Most of the women interviewed considered their lack of language skills and education as a major barrier to using the computer more frequently (Schreiner 1998).

Community learning centers may also provide some access to telephone and computer communication. These centers and the study groups that they support are a common feature of distance education provision around the world. They appear to provide the type of learning opportunity that seems suited to the learning styles many women prefer: that of connectedness and mutual support (Kirkup and von Prümmer 1990; Grace 1991). The community-based approach to learning that community learning centers make possible may also be of particular appeal to women whose communities constitute their primary reference point and support network (Spronk and Radtke 1988).

Learning centers are by no means a guaranteed solution to the problem of making learning technologies readily accessible to women, however. Many women are confined to their homes because of religious and cultural proscription or the demands of childrearing and housework. Even when leaving the house is not proscribed, husbands may disallow such privileges for a mere "women's meeting." And even if women are allowed to attend, they will probably find transport difficult and expensive. Moreover, they may find little moral support in their immediate environment for what they are trying to do. Husbands and other family members and friends may resent or mock a woman for the time she spends on her learning endeavors and put all manner of barriers – subtle and not so subtle – in her way.

Setting up learning centers also entails considerable costs, which may be difficult for governments, communities, or self-help groups to afford. Centers have to be built, bought, or rented. They need to be equipped and staffed with people who know how to make them woman-friendly. For example, programs need to be in place for building women's skills in using these technologies and building their confidence in themselves as competent learners. Centers also need to be maintained, as does the equipment, not a trivial detail when funds and expertise are scarce. In addition, centers need to be numerous enough to be genuinely available to the women whom they target as their learners. Child care or creche facilities would be an added bonus. Such learning center schemes do exist in the developing world, but almost all get their start from donor funding and all too often die from underfunding and neglect once the donor money is exhausted. For example, the telecenter studied by Schreiner (1998) was funded for its first year by the government from donor-supplied grants in the expectation that in a year's time revenues would more than cover costs. Well into its second year of operation, however, income was still far short of what would be needed for self-sufficiency. It is all too easy to get excited about the potential offered by a network of truly community-based and community-operated centers, but it is quite another matter to build a sustainable base for funding for them.

In addition to costs, however, there is the issue of the choices that need to be made. Faced with scarce resources, decision-makers need to make sure that the technologies on which they choose to spend those resources are the best buy. Is it the wisest choice, for example, to spend £1,000 on a computer, another £80 or so a month for an Internet connection and telephone line, and another £20 or so a month on fuel for the generator needed to provide a constant supply of power, when that same money could provide 1,000 sets of materials for women who have just learned to read so that they can continue to build their skills and put them to use? Our enthusiasm for a particular technology may blind us to other possibilities that may be much more appropriate to the real and felt needs of the women learners for whom they are intended.

An effective way of determining which choices of technology are most appropriate is to involve the women themselves in making the choices. This may seem obvious, especially in the light of the participatory approaches to development that are currently advocated (see, e.g., Chambers 1993). The benefit to marginalized women of such holistic and participative methods is clear nonetheless. By being supported in making choices, women become more fully agents of their own development rather than victims of it. In order to make this happen, those of us who are privileged to work with these women and with the organizations that support them must stay alert to our own assumptions and their effects, and be humble in the face of the issues these women must deal with and the strength with which they face them.

Lessons to remember

1   Beware of our own assumptions. They limit what we see and what we will acknowledge.
2   Recognize the influence of poverty on people's lives. They need to spend their days doing chores that help sustain them and their families. Time is a precious commodity for them also.
3   Check that learners have access to site-based group activities. Access can be affected by social status, religion, and tradition as well as by money, time, and other family responsibilities.
4   Consider the use of community centers that are local and community-owned and operated, but recognize that they are difficult to sustain on fees alone.
5   Seek the participation of learners in choices about learning. Their involvement is the only way to develop ownership, control, and participation in their future.

References

Benería, L. and Roldan, M. (1987) *The Crossroads of Class and Gender: Industrial Homework, Subcontracting, and Household Dynamics in Mexico City.* Chicago: University of Chicago Press.

Chambers, R. (1993) *Rural Development: Putting the Last First.* Harlow: Longman.

Grace, M. (1991) "Gender Issues in Distance Education: A Feminist Perspective," in T. Evans (ed.) *Beyond the Text: Contemporary Writing on Distance Education.* Geelong: Deakin University Press.

Kabeer, N. (1994) *Reversed Realities: Gender Hierarchies in Development Thought.* London: Verso.

Kirkup, G. and Von Prümmer, C. (1990) "Support and Connectedness: The Needs of Women Distance Education Students," *Journal of Distance Education,* 5, 2, 9–31.

Mbilinyi, M. (1984) *Cooperation or Exploitation? Experiences of Women's Initiatives in Tanzania.* Geneva: ILO.

Mies, M. (1982) *The Lace Makers of Narsapur: Indian Housewives Produce for the World Market.* London: Zed Books.

Oppong, C. (ed.) (1983) *Female and Male in West Africa.* London: Allen and Unwin.

Schreiner, H. (1998) "Rural Women, Development, and Telecommunications: A Pilot Programme in South Africa," in C. Sweetman (ed.) *Gender and Technology.* Oxford: Oxfam.

Sen, A. (1990) "More than 100 Million Women are Missing," *New York Review of Books,* 20, 61–64.

Sen, G. and Grown, C. (1987) *Development, Crises and Alternative Visions: Third World Women's Perspectives.* New York: Monthly Review Press.

Spronk, B. and Radtke, D. (1988) "Problems and Possibilities: Canadian Native Women in Distance Education," in K. Faith (ed.) *Toward New Horizons for Women in Distance Education: International Perspectives*. London: Routledge.

United Nations Development Programme (UNDP) (1997) *Human Development Report 1997*. Oxford: Oxford University Press.

United Nations Development Programme (UNDP) (1999) *Human Development Report 1999*. Oxford: Oxford University Press.

United Nations Development Programme (UNDP) (2000) *Human Development Report 2000*. Oxford: Oxford University Press.

Vital Signs, annual publication from the Worldwatch Institute. Washington, DC: www.worldwatch.org.

3 Public and institutional policy interplay: Canadian examples

*Judith M. (Judy) Roberts,
Erin M. Keough, and Lucille Pacey*

Introduction

> The transition to a knowledge-based economy is a global phenomenon. To remain competitive countries must enable their labor forces to acquire and upgrade the skills necessary to work with the ever-changing technologies being used in the production of goods and services. Technological developments are creating new jobs, markets and business, and consequently are increasing the demand for continuing education and training.
>
> (Industry Canada 1998: 6)

As Canada shifts from a resource-based to a knowledge-based economy, the expectations and pressures placed on formal education systems to deliver relevant, current, and industry-related education and training increase. Governments see a clear link between a strong, prosperous economy and educational systems outputs, and in doing so they must deal with several key policy areas: four in our opinion. Institutions also face several key policy areas: we see five. In this chapter we discuss both groups of policy areas in the context of today's societal and educational shifts. We believe that if the policy areas are not adequately addressed, any effective use of information and communications technologies (ICTs) may be compromised.

Our thinking comes from our experiences as leaders of distance education institutions, consortia, and interactive networks in the Canadian provinces of British Columbia, Ontario, and Newfoundland and Labrador. We have worked as line managers in organizations, as consultants to national and international public and private-sector organizations, and as leaders of the Canadian Association for Distance Education (www.cade-aced.ca). We have, therefore, experienced the intersection of public and institutional policy and seen how the two affect open and distance education and the application of ICTs.

We are also influenced by major writers in the field of public policy. Dohmen (1996), Danely-Gellman and Fetzner (1998), and Hanna (1998) build a scaffolding for our thinking. These researchers, as well as Matthews

(1998), give excellent starting points for understanding the policy issues we raise here.

One Canadian national agenda promotes the deployment of information communication technologies (ICTs) and access to them for learning, for creating new knowledge industries, and for promoting wider access to information. Once information is more easily available through ICTs, those who promote this agenda assume that a more informed citizenry will gradually shift the locus of control, decentralizing many aspects of everyday life ranging from learning to participation in democratic processes. However, federal telecommunications policy and Canada's Connecting Canadians initiative have opened the doors to an alternative scenario, to a different mix of players in education, for example, community development workers, volunteers, and ICT providers. Although infrastructure deployment falls under Canadian federal government jurisdiction, education is the responsibility of the provincial governments. Two levels of public policy thus affect distance education.

Industrialized countries now experience a demographic shift toward an older population at the same time as they become more diverse because of immigration and workforce mobility. The pace of change has accelerated compared with the past, thus shortening planning and implementation cycles. At the same time, public funding of education has decreased. Distance education stakeholders, like colleagues in many other sectors, are challenged by these developments and forced to examine their core strengths and their traditional way of doing business.

Governments formulate the public policy frameworks within which public and private institutions function. Today governments are developing many new policies to cope with the changes we describe above. We believe that the four key government policy areas that most affect open and distance education institutions, organizations, and ourselves as practitioners are decentralized decision-making, the link between education and economic development, universal access to ICTs, and the need to maximize operational efficiency.

To illustrate our arguments we examine five institutional policy areas in the context of two Canadian case studies: Contact North/Contact Nord and TéléÉducation NB TeleEducation. We know these two cases well (Judy worked closely with each as a senior staff member and consultant respectively). Both organizations have won international recognition as an example of best practice, and each has worked in close partnership with both governments and educational institutions. Our summaries of the cases use data supplied in mid-2000 and verified by each organization's senior staff member.

Case studies

Contact North/Contact Nord (CN/CN) hired its first staff in February 1987 after a brief planning process launched by the Ontario government's May

1986 announcement that Can$20 million would be made available for a four-year pilot project in distance education in northern Ontario (Jean-Louis 2000). Through a directed partnership process initiated by the Ministry of Education and the Ministry of Colleges and Universities, Letters of Agreement were signed between the government and four northern post-secondary institutions. At the end of the pilot phase in 1990, CN/CN became an established government program.

Throughout 1987–95 management and operations were contracted to four northern Ontario postsecondary institutions: Laurentian University and Cambrian College in the northeast and Lakehead University and Confederation College in the northwest. A Letter of Agreement governed the 1987–90 period; a formal contract was signed for the 1990–95 period. The four contractors, partners in the secondary sector, functioned by consensus and were advised by appropriate pluralistic advisory committees representing stakeholders.

Following a Sunset Review (i.e., end-of-project assessment) in 1995, major changes were introduced in CN/CN's governance model and its service focus. It is now an incorporated, not-for-profit entity with a 13-member board that is drawn from the community served by CN/CN: for example, small and remote communities, Francophones, Aboriginal peoples, the community at large, all levels of education, and the private sector. The service focus has shifted from a single emphasis on the formal education sector to inclusion of the whole community (e.g., social services, health, etc.) and the private sector. Its strategic public-sector partners are 100 communities, northern Ontario universities and colleges, northern Ontario school boards, and the Government of Ontario. Its strategic private-sector partners are ADCOM Inc., Bell Canada, and IBM Canada. In 1998–99, the most recent year for which statistics were available in July 2000, CN/CN distributed 470 courses.

Contact North/Contact Nord now has three main divisions. Its network supports audio, audiographic, computer, and videoconferencing in 145 access sites in 101 communities across northern Ontario (an area of approximately 880,000 km^2). Internet facilities are also available. Its Centre of Distance Education for Secondary Schools focuses on specific access and technological challenges for secondary schools throughout northern Ontario. Its Centre for Innovation in Learning offers a variety of programs to help educators and trainers select and use advanced learning technologies effectively. It also hosts two learning and training labs, of which the 14 private-sector partners include TeleSat Canada, Avalon Information Technologies Inc., Cancom, and Virtual Learning Environments Inc. The labs allow educators and trainers to beta-test and evaluate new and emerging learning technologies. In February 2000 ADCOM Video-conferencing and CN/CN launched the Ontario Centre of Excellence in Videoconferencing with a view to enhancing program delivery, research, and evaluation.

The primary source of funding for CN/CN has been the Ontario government. After increasing funding over the years to keep pace with growing network use, the government froze the budget in 1997. In response, CN/CN continues to streamline its operations and diversify its sources of revenue.

Although it was not directly administered by CN/CN, a Northern Distance Education Fund existed as part of the Ontario government's distance education funding allocation for northern Ontario. Institutions could apply in partnership for up to 50 percent of the costs of redesigning entire degree, certificate, or diploma programs to a distance education format. Between 1986 and 1997 it disbursed Can$9.6 million to 37 projects (MacPherson 1999).

TéléÉducation NB TeleEducation (TENB) was created in 1993 to provide community-based access to training, information, and other learners' support services for the only officially bilingual province of Canada, New Brunswick (73,000 km^2, McGreal 2000). TéléÉducationNB facilitates the delivery of distance learning programs developed by New Brunswick schools, colleges, universities, and private trainers and is a prime vehicle for promoting the province's social policy goal of access to learning opportunities in all regions and the economic goal of promoting the growth of the advanced training technology sector of the provincial economy.

Originally established as a unit in the Department of Advanced Education and Labour, which has since been restructured, TENB is now part of the Department of Education. An Advisory Board appointed by the Minister meets regularly and makes recommendations on directions for the network. The board includes representatives of different government departments, all the provincial universities and other public higher education institutions, the health sector, and the private sector. There is a 50–50 balance between the public and private sectors on the board.

Adult education has been TENB's primary focus. From 1993 to 1998 there was consistent growth in the number of students making use of its audio-graphic network from 832 students in the first year in 44 courses to 4,817 in more than 124 courses. It is significant that more than 200,000 out-of-province students now use the Internet to take courses from New Brunswick-based training companies and institutions. TéléÉducationNB uses the Connect NB Branché community access sites (over 200 learning centers in over 150 communities) to facilitate access in the province.

TéléÉducationNB also supports the TeleCampus, an online portal for students, instructors, and administrators that has information about distance learning and links to other distance learning Web sites. The TeleCampus Online Course Directory is considered the most comprehensive listing of online courses available on the World Wide Web. As of July 2000 it listed more than 28,000 courses from 32 countries.

Funding of Can$10.5 million for the first four years of TENB's existence was provided by the federal and provincial governments through a

Canada-New Brunswick COOPERATION Agreement on Entrepreneurship and Human Resource Development. Until 1999 TENB was funded through the Department of Education and the federal-provincial Regional Economic Development Agreement. At the time of writing, new funding arrangements are being discussed. Special initiatives are funded from other sources: for example, the TeleCampus Online Course Directory is funded by agencies such as the World Bank, the Commonwealth of Learning, and the Consortium International Francophone de Formation à Distance.

A Program Development Fund (PDF) was established in 1993 to provide public institutions and private training companies with incentive funding to support their development of quality distance education courses and programs. Furthermore, TENB and PDF are key elements in the province's economic development strategy of incubating the advanced training technology (ATT) sector. TéléÉducationNB targeted the needs of this sector and used the PDF to play a catalytic role in the development of new companies specializing in learning and training technologies. This ATT sector contains more than 60 ATT companies, which employ over 1,000 people, and is growing at the rate of 30 percent annually.

Policy areas

We believe that by creating and continuing to support these two networks, the governments of Ontario and New Brunswick have (implicitly or explicitly) implemented the four policy priorities we mention above; that is, they have decentralized decision-making, linked education to economic development, tried to provide universal access to ICTs, and sought to maximize operational efficiency through partnerships.

Once CN/CN and TENB began to function within these government policy priorities, a number of institutional issues arose. We therefore analyze how the five key institutional policy areas played out. They are organizational model, mandate, resources, consultation, and technology.

Organizational model

We understand *organizational models* as the structure and form in which policy is implemented.

One of the policy priorities for the governments of Ontario and New Brunswick in establishing CN/CN and TENB was to provide their citizens with increased access to education and training. Addressing the access issue involves many other factors, for example, learner support systems, connectivity, and staff roles. Such interdependency offered these two governments some choices for the organizational model they could use to realize their policy objectives. We now examine four features of organizational models: their implementation process, the resulting outcome, their responsiveness to change and their responsiveness to their stakeholders.

The implementation process

By using a directed partnership model to implement CN/CN, we believe the government of Ontario made a strategic investment in infrastructure with minimal stakeholder consultation. Indeed, we would argue that this directed model continued until 1995. Despite an extraordinary "good faith" effort by the four contractors to manage the project to serve all stakeholders, the only formal structure that allowed any stakeholder input was a set of advisory committees.

The government of New Brunswick, on the other hand, undertook a two-year strategic planning process in which a cross-sectoral committee was established, a literature research was conducted, the results of a needs assessment process were documented, and broad consultation was undertaken with stakeholders who were not already represented on the committee. The government thus made a strategic investment in infrastructure after a more pluralistic consultation process than was used in Ontario. However, we would argue that New Brunswick stakeholders have had the same limited participation in governance as did Ontario stakeholders until 1995, as New Brunswick stakeholders participate as governance advisors, not decision-makers.

The outcome

Despite the different implementation processes and resulting organizational structures, the mandate of both organizations continues to be similar, that is, to provide access to education and training. Both networks were authorized to establish learning centers throughout their mandated geographic areas and to distribute courses created by existing universities, colleges, and schools. We believe that it is important to recognize that a policy objective can be achieved through a number of different implementation mechanisms.

Responsiveness to change

Both governments and their partnering stakeholders have responded to changed circumstances. After essentially renewing the organizational structure in 1990, the government of Ontario, after broad stakeholder consultation in the Sunset Review process in 1995, then transformed CN/CN into an incorporated, not-for-profit entity with its own board. The government of New Brunswick also responded to changing circumstances by modifying TENB's reporting structure in government. Although originally reporting to the Ministry of Advanced Education and Labour, TENB is now part of the Ministry of Education.

Mandate

We define *mandate*, which is our second institutional policy area, as an agency's core function, its reason for existing, that clearly defines what it does, whom it serves, and how it delivers its services. Even if an organization believes that what it does can remain valid and stable in a changed environment, it seems to us that no institution can assume that other components of its mandate (e.g., its target groups and services) will enjoy similar stability. The operations of TENB and CN/CN feature issues of clarity and partnerships that we believe may apply to other distance education organizations.

Clarity

A critical challenge for the New Brunswick and Ontario governments, in our opinion, was how to realize their own policy objectives by creating new organizational structures without threatening the roles and responsibilities of existing institutions. Their solution was to craft clear and distinct mandates for CN/CN and TENB that supplemented and complemented existing institutional mandates. For example, both CN/CN and TENB are responsible for installing and operating interactive networks, staffing and operating community learning centers, and providing instructional design support as necessary to universities, colleges, and other content providers. Course and program content providers retain total control over student admissions, faculty assignment, selection of content, and student evaluation.

Although it was easy to delineate such clear distinctions on paper, it was difficult to maintain them in practice. For example, courses were described as CN/CN courses by learners, presumably because learners went to CN/CN access centers to take the courses. So it was important for CN/CN staff to stress that a course that they helped deliver was in fact a Laurentian University or a Confederation College course. The ability to define accurately and explain core mandates and areas of distinct responsibility allows institutions to identify useful partnerships.

Partnerships

The organizational models for CN/CN and TENB depended on strong, effective partnerships to realize their mission. There were slight differences, however, in the nature of the partnerships. For example, TENB's terms of reference empowered it to partner with both the public and private sectors, whereas CN/CN initially could partner only with the public sector. Other types of partnerships exist in Canada's distance education environment. For example, the TeleLearning Network of Centres of Excellence (TL-NCE) is a research partnership, whereas the Canadian Network for Advanced Research in Industry and Education Inc. (CANARIE) is a more technology-oriented collaborative business structure.

Resources

In this our third institutional policy area, *resources* include the staff, the infra-structures (e.g., telecommunication, space), and the funds needed if the institution is to implement its mandate effectively. The revenue base for distance education has traditionally consisted of government funding, tuition, and "other" funds. Decreasing support from governments now challenges the composition of this funding model and leads to the key question of "Who pays for what?" The challenge of reduced public-sector funding and the development of successful compensatory strategies are not unique in our own experience or to the two case studies we review in this chapter.

Reduced public funding

Governments are reducing funding to public institutions and expecting them to become more entrepreneurial. In order to effect the desired policy objectives such as providing greater access to ICTs, linking education to economic development, and encouraging private–public partnerships, governments are creating strategic funding programs to encourage targeted change (rather than providing general funding for unspecified change).

As well as more recent initiatives such as CANARIE, CN/CN and TENB have program development funds, but they set conditions such as requiring that applications be accepted only if they are submitted by partners, not by a single sponsor.

New funding sources

Not only are distance education institutions using new targeted funding sources in response to government priorities, they are also seeking new sources of funds that meet their own needs. For example, many institutions are increasing their efforts to recruit more international students and are marketing and brokering their courses and services more aggressively than in the past. We believe that many institutions are also shifting a greater proportion of their costs to learners, using measures such as increasing tuition fees, making a telecommunications assessment, and/or requiring students to have their own computers and Internet access. At the same time institutions are reducing spending wherever possible and changing both how services are offered and the mix of services offered.

Consultation

We use the term *consultation*, which is our fourth policy area, to mean active encouragement of input from stakeholders in planning, implementing, and evaluating policy and practice. Many would argue that ICT deployment broadens the definition of an institution's stakeholders and enhances their ability to participate in the consultation process. For example, both CN/CN and TENB use their own technical networks to hold board and advisory committee meetings.

We believe there is a growing expectation that citizens will have a more substantial voice in government decisions that affect their lives. In Canada this assertion applies in the health and education sectors. Although it is incumbent on public agencies to consult more broadly, it is also important for stakeholders actively to influence the policy decision-making of institutions and governments. Educational stakeholders in Canada have, for example, significantly influenced the public policy environment of agencies such as the Canadian Radio-Television and Telecommunications Commission (CRTC). An instance of this is that we have negotiated a new customer group that includes education, health, and public libraries. No longer are educational stakeholders treated as a business with the accompanying rates; lower rates that recognize the public good addressed by these agencies can be negotiated. Another example applies at the institutional level: distance education students and faculty can influence institutional policy through such activities as presenting briefs to university senates, participating on boards, or volunteering as distance education part-time representatives on student councils.

Technology

In *technology*, our fifth policy area, we include all ICTs that historically have been distinct hardware and software networks. It is commonplace now to acknowledge the phenomenon of their rapid convergence and the emergence of a globally networked information environment.

The ICT infrastructure, its costs, and availability are critical to the implementation of institutional mandates and of government policy. This key issue was addressed by CN/CN and TENB in unique ways: CN/CN through a strategic government partnership and TENB by partnering with the telecommunications provider to influence policy.

Partnerships

Contact North/Contact Nord acted as a catalyst to create new partnerships with government. For example, when its long-distance communications costs increased significantly as more educational partners delivered courses over its network, CN/CN negotiated access to the Ontario government's telecommunications network in order to gain access to a lower long-distance tariff.

Policy interpretation

Telecommunications vendors in Canada are highly regulated by government policy. Nevertheless, NBTel (the provincial telephone company) took a risk and agreed to set an educational rate for TENB well before the national regulator, the CRTC, did. In effect, NBTel found a way to interpret broadly the then-current telecommunications policy. Avoiding a narrow interpretation of policy also enabled the Ontario government to give CN/CN access to unused government telecommunications network facilities to reduce its long-distance communications costs.

Policy lessons learned

We begin our conclusion with five key policy-related lessons of our own, then offer several key guidelines for open and distance education practitioners and policy developers.

1   It is challenging to categorize policies into neat conceptual groupings, and we have made it look much neater than it is in real life! For example, we categorize the issue of partnership under mandate and technology, but many colleagues may categorize it under organizational structure.
2   We have to adjust to unexpected changes when the pace of those changes increases, but the time available for developing appropriate policy responses decreases. In North America it is usual for governments to seek stakeholders' inputs into the development and implementation of policy, as Ontario and New Brunswick have done. However, in being responsive to stakeholders, governments need to ensure that their policy changes enable all the relevant players, not constrain them.
3   It is important to examine the possible impact of the new financial environment on learners. Many changes appear to involve shifting a greater proportion of educational costs to learners. We believe that one of the key ethical issues in the institutional use of online delivery methods in particular is the question of whether students pay a higher proportion of the cost of their education than they would if they studied on campus.
4   It is critically important to assess the appropriateness of organizational structures. In earlier distance education contexts, for example, the traditional structure and form of university policy and practice were applied to the offering of correspondence courses. Today, as many colleagues would argue, advances in digital networks create a need for new organizational structures that can function effectively in a globally networked society.
5   The complex interplay between education, economic development, and ICT infrastructure deployment means that institutions and practitioners cannot remain ignorant of or isolated from the public and institutional policy processes that we illustrate. The public policy literature is not, we believe, familiar to many of our colleagues in open and distance education. Educational leaders need to be well informed about the technical process of public policy development and the various frameworks used to analyze public policy.

Let us suggest three initial ways in which distance education practitioners and administrators can become more actively involved in the public policy process. The first is to recognize and anticipate the linkage between educational policy, financial policy, and telecommunications policy and become more informed about the technical process of public policy development and the frameworks used to analyze public policy. Policies in one area can affect the output in other policy areas. Policy frameworks typically are complex, but at a minimum they should express the intent, provide evidence of need, demonstrate the desired direction, define targets, and define the scope of the needed outcomes. Administrators and practitioners alike should expect to see these expressions in a well-prepared policy document. An easy-to-read and still relevant foundation document for anyone new to the field of public policy practice is *Public Policy Analysis* by Pal (1992).

The second strategy is for administrators to analyze the key policy drivers. These are educational objectives (including relevance and currency of quality assurance measures), cultural and social concerns, and economic competitiveness. Developing policy targeted toward educational and social reform may result in economic benefits, but if we pay attention to the economic agenda at the start of the process we can promote a more holistic approach to policy development.

The third way of participating in the public policy process, at either the government level or the institutional level, is to understand fully the various stakeholder groups, their roles, and the structures through which they are consulted. A classic resource in this area is *Politics and Public Policy* by Pross (1992). Distance educators have recognized the difficulty of funding and maintaining policy agendas that are formed around goals of social access and the common good. An ICT infrastructure, for example, is at risk of becoming a competitive advantage only for financially and socially elite groups of people. To minimize this kind of result, distance educators are challenged to become involved in the policy development process at its input stage. Regular monitoring of the policy landscape and early interventions can then result in more effective outcomes.

Because no single formula works across every policy environment and every institutional culture, our challenge is to understand the basic elements of a policy framework, maintain regular monitoring processes, and be clear about the desired outcomes for the field of distance education.

References

Canadian Network for Advanced Research in Industry and Education (CANARIE) Inc. Online. Available: http://www.canarie.ca.

Connecting Canadians. Online. Available: http://www.connect.gc.ca.

Contact North/Contact Nord. Online. Available: http://www.cnorth.edu.on.ca.

Danely-Gellman, B. and Fetzner, M.J. (1998) "Asking the Really Tough Questions:

Policy Issues for Distance Learning." Online. *Online Journal of Distance Learning Administration*, 1, 1. Available: http://www.westga.edu/~distance/danley11.html.

Dohmen, G. (1996) *Life Long Learning: Guidelines for a Modern Education Policy*. Bonn: Federal Ministry of Education, Science, Research and Technology.

Hanna, D.E. (1998) "Higher Education in an Era of Digital Competition: Emerging Organizational Models," *Journal of Asynchronous Learning Networks*, 2, 1. Online. Available: http://www.aln.org/alnweb/journal/jaln.htm.

Industry Canada (1998) "Report of the Panel on Smart Communities." David Johnson (chair). Ottawa: Information Distribution Centre, Communications Branch, Industry Canada. Online. Available: http://smartcommunities.ic.gc.ca.

Jean-Louis, M. (2000) Personal communication, July.

MacPherson, B. (1999) Personal communication, November.

Matthews, D. (1998) "The Transformation of Higher Education Through Information Technology, Implications for State Higher Education Finance Policy." Online. Available: http://www.educause.edu/nlii/keydocs/finance.html.

McGreal, R. (2000) Personal communication, July.

Pal, L.A. (1992) *Public Policy Analysis*. Toronto: Nelson Canada.

Pross, P. (1992) *Politics and Public Policy* (2nd edn). Toronto: Oxford University Press.

TéléÉducationNB TeleEducation (TENB). Online. Available:http://teleeducation. nb.ca.

TeleLearning Network of Centres of Excellence (TL-NCE). Online. Available: http://www.telelearn.ca.

4 Getting the systems right: Experience at the University of the West Indies

Christine Marrett and Claudia Harvey

The University of the West Indies (UWI) is a three-campus, regional institution serving 16 countries in the English-speaking Caribbean.[1] The campuses are the Mona Campus in Jamaica, the St Augustine Campus in Trinidad and Tobago, and the Cave Hill Campus in Barbados. The countries served are island states separated by the Caribbean Sea, with small populations ranging from 5,000 in the volcano-ravaged island of Montserrat to some 2.5 million in Jamaica.

In this chapter we list the significant technological and administrative steps taken to adopt distance education at UWI, outline recent challenges, and end with the key lessons we have learned through direct experience with technology-mediated distance education.

The history of distance education at UWI began in 1978 with a two-month pilot involving three countries, followed by a three-year feasibility study, which in turn led to a three-year experimental project. Finally, the university established a center organized as a full strategic arm of the whole university system. So important was distance education considered for the last phase that it was incorporated as one of three key functional areas operating under university-wide policy boards: graduate studies, undergraduate studies, and noncampus and distance education. Over the past 22 years of this activity, the challenges of implementing distance education were based in UWI's changing context from traditional single-mode (face to face only) to dual-mode operations (face-to-face and distance modes) distributed over developing countries.

Christine Marrett has been closely involved with managing the evolution of distance education at the UWI since 1982; Claudia Harvey was involved first as a course developer in the early 1980s and then as Director of the UWI Distance Education Centre (UWIDEC) in its first year of operation, 1996–97.

Significant steps

In 1978, with funding from the United States Agency for International Development (USAID), UWI investigated the use of telecommunications for improving service to its clientele throughout the Caribbean region. A two-month experiment, known as Project Satellite, was launched that entailed one-way, full-motion video from the Mona Campus in Jamaica (via an ATS-6 NASA satellite) to the Cave Hill Campus in Barbados, with return audio (via an ATS-3 satellite). St Lucia joined the system during the final two weeks. The educational programs and discussion seminars, which included both the university and the extramural community, focused on rural medical care, agricultural research, the nurse-practitioner program, family life education in schools, the education of the deaf, and early childhood education. The UWI staff produced the programs in collaboration with a television station, the Jamaica Broadcasting Corporation, and agencies such as the Goddard Space Flight Centre, the University of Miami, and the Solar Energy Research Centre. The satellite-based system was used also for university administrative meetings: a real advantage for the multicountry, multicampus context of UWI. Project Satellite demonstrated the potential for using distance technology in a Caribbean educational environment. Still to be tested, however, was its feasibility for sustained use in terms of program production, costs, applicability beyond the three test countries, and its usefulness for students in formal educational settings.

The second significant step toward the implementation of distance education emerged from the interest generated by Project Satellite. The USAID-funded three-year Caribbean Regional Communications Study (CARCOST – 1979–80, 1981–82) examined the feasibility of interactive distance teaching and other types of teleconferences for education and public service in the Caribbean. The study included an experiment with distance teaching between three sites in Jamaica using the telephone system. The UWI staff visited several distance teaching projects and, with consultants as needed, examined the potential for using communication technologies to design solutions for selected Caribbean problems. They also demonstrated the use of emerging technologies (such as freeze-frame television and facsimile transmission) and maintained close connections with other regional institutions and ministries of agriculture, education, and health.

At this phase of development, potential major stakeholders began to work together. Given the small populations of the countries, their relative isolation, and their limited human and financial resources, the CARCOST study recommended that sharing the operation and cost of telecommunications could effectively satisfy the collective needs of these populations. It was suggested that a real-time interactive system, rather than a broadcast system, would meet the needs of potential participants. The need to develop simultaneously other course material formats such as print, audiovisual, and other media was also emphasized. Support for implementing the recommendations of the study was solicited from the political leaders in the Caribbean countries through the Caribbean Community (CARICOM),[2] particularly from those in the health, education, and agriculture sectors.

Following CARCOST, negotiations between UWI and USAID resulted in the third step: a three-year project beginning in 1982 to establish an interactive audiographic teleconference network known as the UWI Distance Teaching Experiment (UWIDITE). Because the only satellite available was the ATS-3 and its future was uncertain, and because the cost of the receiver terminals was not falling as rapidly as anticipated, the teleconference network was designed to use the regional telephone system rather than to link directly to a satellite. Equipment (for five centers in the three campuses and in Dominica and St Lucia) included microphones and speakers, a telewriter system to simulate the use of a blackboard, and a slow-scan system for transmitting still images. The slow-scan technology was later discontinued after a new telewriter system was developed that offered essentially the same function. In addition to teleconferences as the main medium of instruction, extensive print materials were provided for students; these were important because some sites did not have fully fledged libraries that could supply adequate reading materials for courses. The program areas for this activity included education, social, and medical sciences, as identified in the findings of the CARCOST project.

At the end of the three-year project in 1985, UWI assumed budgetary responsibility for UWIDITE, which led to a name change: the UWI Distance Teaching Enterprise. Not only had distance education been successfully implemented in an experimental phase, but it was at the University to stay and was expanding.

As funding became available from various sources, additional centers were added to the network. In Jamaica, sites were established with local and international funding and help from community institutions such as high schools, a community college, and a teachers' college, which provided housing for the teleconference rooms. The host institution for each site also provided staff support.

The number of programs offered was increased, and several of these were not core faculty programs, but programs of special centers in the university (e.g., Caribbean Child Development Centre) or regional organizations (e.g., Caribbean Food and Nutrition Institute, Caribbean Epidemiological Centre). Thus the UWIDITE system became a key contributor to continuing education activity in the Caribbean.

The core of the distance education program during the late 1980s revolved around the UWIDITE office and what became in effect its outreach arm: the teleconference sites located in the university centers throughout the region. Although each academic faculty maintained responsibility for course content, examinations, and all substantive matters, it became clear that UWI distance education had become synonymous with the UWIDITE office. As a result, UWIDITE became all things to distance education students. Too often students were automatically referred by UWI staff to the UWIDITE office once they identified themselves as distance education students, no matter what was the issue – financial, academic, or other – and regardless of who should most appropriately handle the matter. An associated problem was that the distance education program was perceived as an additional rather than a core responsibility for different sections of the university. For example, distance students were considered as somewhat different from on-campus students, with the result that often administrative matters for distance education students were dealt with only after campus-based student matters (such as selection of applicants and examination processing) had been resolved.

This perception of difference added a layer of meaning to the reactions of faculty members regarding development of course material. Because the lecturers would often have regular on-campus course loads, many regarded their distance education responsibilities, including the development of materials, as an additional burden. Also evident, as Lalor and Marrett reported, were skeptical attitudes from some who "thought it a waste of human effort on speculative, high technology, unlikely to further the cause of education in the Caribbean" (1986: 11). Some faculties saw the provision of print materials as "spoonfeeding," expressed concern about copyright, and argued that the preparation of the print material was not at all easy: "It is a time consuming chore which already busy people can justifiably be reluctant to undertake, the more so since the lead times were much too short" (1986: 25). In addition, because a real-time interactive system was in use, access to distance programs now depended on the availability of space in centers that housed the interactive technology. This presented an ironic but real challenge, because other technologies, for example print, had "untied" distance education activity from fixed, particular spaces. Greater demand for courses, as well as competition from several other providers who were becoming active in the region, now challenged this concept of a center-based distance education system.

Despite all the various challenges, thousands of students gained access to the UWI because a distance-mode option was available. Advocates of distance education grew in number.

Then UWI undertook a major strategic planning exercise to reexamine its relationship with its stakeholders and to assess its goals, programs, and structures. Among the key stakeholders – who were demanding that distance education courses be further expanded – were the noncampus countries and also the noncampus communities in its largest campus country, Jamaica. UWI planners also faced constraints on physical expansion, the possibilities offered by just-available newer technologies, and the international expansion of distance education. In 1992 the university declared itself to be a dual-mode institution, with the intention that:

- students will be able to access programs by face-to-face or distance delivery or a combination of both
- staff will treat the development and delivery of programs by distance as an integral part of their work and have this suitably recognized by their faculties

- student-centeredness, quality and cost effectiveness will be hallmarks of all University programs
- sufficient resources, including recognition of academic effort, will be allocated by administration and faculties to enable the attainment of these goals (UWIDEC 1996).

Accordingly, the university established the UWI Distance Education Centre (UWIDEC, www.uwicentre.edu.jm/~uwidec/) in 1996, which, with the School of Continuing Studies and the Tertiary Level Institutions Unit, became one of three directorates of the Board for Non-Campus Countries and Distance Education. The UWIDEC now operates as a facilitating unit in the university, assisting faculties to develop and implement distance education programs. The control of academic content and decisions about which programs should be offered remain the domain of the respective academic faculty. Inside UWIDEC, campus-based curriculum development specialists, editors, production assistants, and a graphic artist work with faculty members to plan and develop the programs and program materials.

To resolve the logistical problem of finding enough space for holding audio-conferenced classes, UWIDEC adopted print-based course manuals and readers as the main medium of instruction. Teleconferences and local face-to-face tutorials became supportive elements only for students who had to use essentially self-study methods with the given print-based course materials. This solution caused some difficulties as it placed greater responsibility on students to direct their own learning. Further, it placed great responsibility on staff to prepare the materials, and because no additional staff were made available for this task, it had to be integrated into the workloads of all staff. The consequent problem of how to reward staff who took on these extra duties (e.g., remuneration or extra academic credit) was not quickly resolved, so production of materials remained problematic. Given the problems of rewarding distance work, it is not surprising that some traditional faculty members were reluctant to embrace the distance education initiative articulated by the policy-makers. The following are two examples of faculty members' concerns about copyright and career development.

> Are you saying that when I would have produced the distance education materials, anybody can use them? Am I giving away my intellectual property?
>
> (Harvey and Williams 1996: 23)

> I have been an academic all my life, progressing fairly smoothly and moving up the career path of the University. Why should I get involved in Distance Education, designing and producing learning materials? I see no benefit in it.
>
> (Harvey and Williams 1996: 24)

Recent challenges

By December 1997 UWIDEC believed it was necessary to organize a symposium entitled Distance Education: From Policy to Operation because:

> from speaking with various persons with different roles to play in the implementation of distance education, [there was] a sense that many felt that they were not part of the decision making process and had only been directed to participate.
>
> (UWIDEC 1997: 7)

The symposium enabled staff to discuss the challenges they saw in implementing distance education. One that was repeatedly highlighted was the demand on faculty time for the development and coordination of distance education courses; such demands often competed with the requirements for on-campus teaching and research. The Dean of the Faculty of Arts and Education summarized the reaction thus: "We are all already overworked. It can't be an add-on and therefore we will have to find either additional people to coordinate it, or decide what we are going to drop from our existing system" (UWIDEC 1997: 39).

This tension between the on-campus and distance education systems was further heightened by a challenge perhaps not fully perceived at the time by the university planners: the operations of the distance education initiative enshrined in UWI policy ran counter to existing but different UWI policy initiatives. For example, more autonomy was given to each campus to develop courses, run their own programs, and set different examinations, but it had also been decided that distance students must write the same examination as the on-campus students, thus begging the question: examination of which campus? Because the feasibility of distance education programs depends on numbers, it was not practical to divide distance students by campus. So while dominant UWI policy moved in the direction of greater campus-based autonomy, the policy logic of distance education aimed for greater coordination. The solution might have been to create a fourth, solely distance campus, but with the steady growth of the number of part-time students on campuses, it seemed unlikely that campuses with representatives on the distance education board would welcome an initiative that in effect would increase competition for their own services. The solution reached was to encourage cross-campus collaboration in the development of programs, with students writing the examination of the campus of the particular course coordinator. Distance education students could thus complete programs containing courses drawn from different campuses. They may in effect represent the only genuine university-wide (as against Cave Hill campus, Mona campus or St Augustine campus) students!

A similar problem of relevance was seen in distance education student registration procedures. Registration had been divided among the three campuses according to specific country groupings, but this split registration created a serious challenge with regard to transmitting information to students from the course coordinator responsible for the delivery of the course across the region. A related problem concerned examinations, collecting papers, and later disseminating results: these are channeled through the examination section of the respective campus of student registration. Structures for facilitating collaboration among the faculty members and registries on the three campuses have yet to be finalized. An obvious solution may be to handle much of the communication electronically. However, implementation of this solution demands infrastructural and psychological readiness. The infrastructure – local area networks and wide area networks – is being put in place at a rate that must be acknowledged as slow for the evident needs. And we suspect that much more work needs to be done to achieve the psychological preparedness of those involved in effecting the necessary changes.

With the incorporation of face-to-face tutorials in the distance education courses arose the problem of identifying suitably qualified persons willing to teach in all the countries, especially for the second- and third-level courses of the BSc, for which the tutor needed at least a master's degree. This problem tended to be more severe in the countries with a smaller population base. Conducting practical work (e.g., teaching practice and labs for science courses) presented another challenge not only in terms of human resources, but also of physical lab resources, because not all the sites had the minimum required facilities.

The attitudes of some students also presented challenges. They did not seem to grasp the need for taking personal responsibility for their own learning, using the materials provided and whatever other resources might be available to them in their own countries. They still expected to be "taught" and were upset when the local tutors did not lecture or deliver the entire course to them. These reactions may have been a holdover from the school system based on a pedagogical model (teaching children) through which they had passed. The transition to an andragogical model (helping adults learn, Knowles *et al.* 1998) is not always easy. We have tried to overcome this particular challenge by holding orientation sessions at the start of the academic year. The local tutors and distance education center coordinators are also given suggestions on how to encourage self-directed learning on the part of the students.

It is a financial and technical challenge for UWI to maintain and update audioconference equipment and to expand course delivery and management options to include Web use. The latter necessarily involves using the national telecommunications infrastructure of each participating country; the problem is that each functions at its own level of development and has its own pricing policies. Primus (1998) has described the intraregional infrastructure as "very weak" and points out that more than 50 percent of inter-Caribbean Internet traffic is routed through the United States, resulting in congestion and reduced service levels. Although all the countries have connectivity and offer a full range of Internet services, the main communication pipes serving the region have inadequate capacity and bandwidth, traffic routing is inefficient and the network architecture is not optimized. As a result the service is of low quality and expensive.

(Primus 1988: Web site)

Variations in national infrastructure among the countries also affect the electricity supply (voltage and reliability) and postal service. Electricity supply problems have been solved by the use of transformers and stand-by generators where necessary, and difficulties with the postal service have been sidestepped by using more expensive but more reliable courier services.

The technological and administrative challenges identified above illustrate an interesting dilemma faced when an innovation is institutionalized. On the one hand, governments and other stakeholders demand distance education. University planners and many staff accept the challenge and advocate the distance mode (Howe 1999). Yet the institutional structures seem not to be flexible enough, and the policies are not easily adaptable to the kinds of change required by the dynamics of distance education.

The challenges also highlight the importance of ongoing, internal communication with all stakeholders inside and outside the institution. As technologies and distance education methodologies change and develop, the need for quality educational programs will increase. Political support (in the broadest sense of the word) is critical and will be more easily won and maintained if communication channels between all stakeholders are kept open.

Given the limited resources available in the Caribbean region, collaboration is essential. The expansion of the UWI-based network was facilitated in many instances through input from projects that originated outside the distance education establishment, but that saw the advantages of collaboration in developing the particular program (e.g., the Caribbean Justice Improvement Project).

Despite the challenges we outline, the demand for distance programs and students' enrollment in them continue to grow, with thousands of students throughout the Caribbean – who might not have been able otherwise to access UWI – being offered an opportunity to achieve a university-level education. The performance of these distance education students is also improving (Reviere 1999). Moreover, distance education methodologies are now used to teach on-campus students in foundation courses that have large enrollments.

Key lessons

We conclude with a summary of what we have learned from our extensive experience with implementing the technologies and other elements of distance education services from the University of the West Indies across the Caribbean area.

1   Publicize early successes. Demonstrate that it can be done, and others will be inspired.
2   Be willing to learn from those you teach or orient toward distance-mode activity. Often a fresh perspective can lead to small innovations that make a big difference.
3   Involve both internal and external stakeholders in planning. In a dual or mixed-mode institution, the commitment of staff throughout the whole institution is required to meet production deadlines and to deal with the particular circumstances of the distance education student. External stakeholders need to be convinced of the validity of the offering.
4   Focus on learning objectives, not the technology.
5   Base decisions about the implementation of technology on research into the actual situation. What works in one country may not necessarily work in another.
6   Use training in the use of the technology as an opportunity to underscore good methods for any teaching and learning situations.
7   Accept that it often takes longer to implement technology solutions in the Caribbean than in developed countries.
8   Examine carefully the cost and resource implications of updating the chosen technology.
9   In a dual-mode institution pay careful attention to faculty members' workloads.

Notes

1 Campus countries: Jamaica, Trinidad and Tobago, Barbados.
   Noncampus countries: Anguilla, Antigua and Barbuda, the Bahama Islands, Belize, the British Virgin Islands, the Cayman Islands, Dominica, Grenada, Montserrat, St Kitts and Nevis, St Lucia, St Vincent and the Grenadines, the Turks and Caicos Islands.
2 CARICOM is an intergovernmental grouping of countries within the region and includes most of the countries that support the UWI, as well as Guyana and Suriname.

References

Harvey, C. and Williams, G. (1996) "Using a Stakeholders' Analysis to Plan for Quality Assurance," *Caribbean Curriculum*, 6, 2, 1–33.
Howe, G. (1999) "A Case Study of Cave Hill Faculty Attitudes, Perceptions, Knowledge and Willingness to Participate in the UWI's Distance Education Enterprise," *Caribbean Waves*, 5, 14 (UWIDEC Newsletter).
Knowles, M.S., Holton, E.F., and Swanson, R.A. (1998) *The Adult Learner* (5th edn). Houston, TX: Gulf.
Lalor, G.C. and Marrett, C. (1986) "University of the West Indies Distance Teaching Experiment (UWIDITE) Report." Kingston: University of the West Indies.
Primus, W.J. (1998) "Preliminary Status Report on Information and Communications

Technology (ICT) Infrastructure in the ACS States." Port of Spain: Association of Caribbean States. Online. Available: http://www.acs-aec.org/primus1.html.

Reviere, R. (1999) "DEC Finds Improvement in Student Performance," *Caribbean Waves*, 5, 12.

UWIDEC (1996) "Preamble," in *Distance Education at the University of the West Indies: Statement of Policies, Principles and Procedures, 1997*. Kingston: University of the West Indies.

UWIDEC (1997) "Symposium on Distance Education at the UWI: From Policy to Operation, Report." Kingston: University of the West Indies.

5 Developing course materials: A context of technology constraints

Judith W. Kamau

Introduction

In the last 30 years, distance education in Africa has changed from being perceived by many as second rate to being an acceptable alternative for adults wishing to acquire new qualifications or upgrade their skills without leaving their jobs and their families (Perraton 1993). Distance education generally has enabled African countries to address problems of illiteracy, population growth, agriculture, and health. The use of communication technologies has continuing potential for addressing urgent issues such as the spread of HIV/AIDS, child survival, education, the skyrocketing refugee population, and the democratization of political systems.

Despite this potential, distance education is severely underresourced. Many institutions, particularly dual-mode organizations, lack the necessary human, fiscal, logistical, and material resources needed to offer state-of-the-art delivery and support. In many African countries distance education programs are still tagged as appendages of Institutes of Extra-Mural Studies and Centres of Continuing Education, thus making expansion difficult. This is mainly because the potential offered by distance modes of education is either unknown, misunderstood, or not yet established. Even where it is known the appropriate decision-makers receive little information.

Many of these problems are evident in the development of distance-mode teacher education. As this is my field of practice, I use examples from Kenya and Botswana to describe the constraints in course development, selection and use of appropriate technologies, and provision of learner support services. These constraints have influenced my work over many years, so my frustrations and reflective comments are embedded in the descriptions that follow. First, though, some scene-setting.

Historical background

With the coming of independence for many African countries in the early 1960s, several educational problems were intensified. Many governments faced high illiteracy rates, many expatriate teachers left the continent, and local teachers were academically and professionally underqualified and in need of rapid inservice upgrading. In 1967 the Kenyan government launched a teacher training correspondence program supported by radio. By the time the program closed in 1974, over 7,000 teachers had graduated (Perraton 1993). Meanwhile, however, because of rapidly increasing enrollment in primary schools, the Kenyan government continued to recruit untrained primary schoolteachers who could not enroll in conventional preservice teacher training colleges, and in 1982 teacher training by distance mode was revived to provide training for them.

The Kenyan government replicated this strategy to train teachers to meet other national needs. The teachers in the adult literacy campaign launched in 1978 were insufficiently qualified for the task, so they were trained using distance modes. By 1985 distance modes were also used to upgrade the skills of secondary school diploma holders to the B.Ed. level.

Between 1960 and 1965 the Botswanan government offered distance-mode upgrading for teachers, and students enrolled in institutions in Salisbury (now Harare), the capital of Rhodesia (now Zimbabwe). Following the success of this experiment and to reduce the number of untrained teachers, the Botswanan government launched the Francistown Project between 1968 and 1973, which involved upgrading over 700 untrained teachers through distance education (Mphinyane 1993). These early initiatives led to the establishment of the Botswana College of Distance and Open Learning (BOCODOL) in 1999, the mandate of which is to provide pretertiary programs for the entire nation. Tertiary-level distance education programs are the responsibility of the University of Botswana.

In other present-day contexts across the African continent, many tertiary-level distance education programs are housed in dual-mode institutions where the administration gives first priority to conventional programs with on campus students. Planners and managers of distance education programs must therefore overcome various procedural and attitudinal barriers in order to obtain program approval and financing and to have appropriate administrative policies for their distance students (Odumbe 1998; Dodds *et al.* 1999). For example, regulations designed to provide flexibility for students must be justified, and payment for services rendered by staff from other internal departments must be guaranteed. Other policy constraints often delay development and production of study materials; for example, the Faculty of External Studies at the University of Nairobi has struggled to gain enough autonomy to run its programs more effectively and efficiently (Kamau 1997).

Course development constraints

Using my own experience, I group the key issues into the categories of time requirements, adequate skilled staff, appropriate acquisition of materials, and operational telecommunication infrastructure.

Rarely are course planning, design, and development given the lead time they need. Sometimes political statements precede development and production of materials, and this can lead to hasty procedures that ignore the types and models of learning technologies already in use. As a result, quality assurance is compromised such that study materials need serious revision even before they are distributed. A good example is that of Kenya, where political pronouncements preceded the development of materials for a primary school-teacher upgrading program, training of literacy teachers, and the B.Ed. (arts) program. Consequently, the University of Nairobi (which was to develop and distribute course materials for these three programs) was under strong pressure to meet course delivery deadlines. Often production schedules were not met, which led to high dropout rates, especially in the B.Ed. program.

This six-year program at the University of Nairobi opened its "doors" during school vacations to 600 enthusiastic students in August 1985, using correspondence texts supported by audiocassette tapes and face-to-face tutorials. However, students from remote areas failed to attend tutorials, saying that they had not received the letters in time. By 1990 enrollment had dropped from 600 to 388, the dropouts citing discouragement from the delays in receiving study materials and feedback on assignments and examinations. In 1994 only 250 graduated. Nevertheless, these graduates became a motivating force for the dropouts, and many returned to complete the program. When the program was advertised for the second intake, over 4,000 applications were received for only 1,500 places. To us this was the acid test that indicated that, despite the problems, the B.Ed. program had once again proved the viability of distance education.

The second constraint is the shortage of qualified, multiskilled instructional designers with experience in both distance and classroom teaching. My experience in both Kenya and Botswana is that many subject specialists, content editors, and copy-editors do not combine subject expertise with technological knowledge. Training even one competent instructional designer or production person takes time. And often course development and production of materials are not completed by the deadlines because of delays in transferring drafts between course writers, editors, and word-processors before they are print-ready. Also, part-time writers, reviewers, and copy-editors delay production by missing deadlines, citing lack of time and heavy teaching loads in their parent institutions.

To circumvent constraints in course development and production and expedite implementation of programs, the University of Nairobi between 1986 and 1990 proposed to acquire materials from other institutions to launch a B.Ed. science program. At that time the University of Nairobi had a collaboration agreement with the International Extension College based in the UK, and sample materials were acquired from the Open University (UK). But this plan backfired: the external materials had to be customized to suit the local examination syllabus, and the faculty felt that this task would take longer than developing course materials from scratch. They also feared that acquiring course materials would deny faculty members at the University of Nairobi a chance to develop writing and editing skills and, as a spin-off benefit, hone their distance teaching skills.

Course sharing has succeeded in a few institutions. Between 1992 and 1995 the University of Makerere, Uganda, the Open University of Tanzania, and the Department of Distance Education of the University of Zimbabwe (renamed Zimbabwe Open University in 1999) began distance education programs in record time using materials acquired from the University of Nairobi. Similarly, the Centre for External Studies in the University of Namibia launched programs using study materials from the University of South Africa. These institutions were then able to develop their own course materials while students studied borrowed materials from other institutions. A more recent development is the African Virtual University (AVU), which has sites on many African campuses. Currently, it gives greater access to courses using videoconferencing (VC) via satellite links, thus replicating conventional education approaches without enhancing them (Uys 1999). If the AVU is to have any impact, it must facilitate staff training in its host countries in the skills needed to develop and produce materials in the multimedia, online environments used by its collaborating institutions in the developed world. Currently, the University of Botswana is exploring the possibilities of VC for its own distance programs.

Of course, for any learning technology to be adopted it must be assessed against the resources available to students and service providers. A recent report on telecommunications in the Southern African Development Community (SADC 1998) indicated that many telecommunications networks still use video and less-efficient analog terrestrial networks that already carry heavy economic communications activities, which results in congestion, slow transmission, and inefficient service. Such capacity constraints, coupled with institutional inefficiency, inadequate maintenance of the telecommunications system, low levels of technical skill, and nonstandard equipment and operating procedures among the networks of the region, reinforce the need to standardize telecommunications.

The constraint of diverse equipment is not specific to the SADC region alone; for example, good intentions can lead to logistical difficulties for users. In 1993 the Commonwealth of Learning donated audioconferencing equipment to the University of Nairobi's distance education project so that staff could link the eight study centers throughout Kenya. After installation, the main audiobridge (made in Canada) did not interface with the available telecommunications equipment. Adjustments eventually made the telecommunications system functional, but delayed its application. We seem to need reminding that it is essential to conduct needs assessment surveys to establish what is in current and reliable use before introducing a new technology.

Selection and use of learning technologies

Except for the newly introduced virtual universities in some African countries that apply advanced technology from the developed world, distance education programs in Africa have successfully used the features of print as a learning technology in its own right (Kabonoki 1999; O'Rourke 2001). The materials are supported by educational radio (Maskow 2001), and – where costs allow – audiocassette tapes. Face-to-face contact sessions are often used as an additional learning technology.

To satisfy local examination syllabuses, rather than adapt readily available print-based course materials, many institutions prefer to develop their own. Distance education departments in dual-mode institutions in Kenya and Botswana rely on available academics among the staff to maintain quality and ensure parity of standards as instructors who teach courses in a conventional program become distance mode educators. These people must write distance mode course materials; teach the course during the face-to-face contact sessions; and set and mark assignments, tests, and final examinations. Relying on these academics has become a common strategy at the University of Nairobi and at the University of Botswana, and their initiative in participating in the distance education programs is recognized when they seek career promotion.

To realize economies of scale and develop all the learning technologies appropriately, the universities of Nairobi and Botswana use a team process to coordinate and link expert staff either concurrently or at various stages of course design, materials development, and course delivery. Training for course writers in each team is essential because they must learn the house style for the print materials and the audiocassette tapes. To complete work in time, we calculate timelines for the development and production of materials and pass these on to writers and editors. Nevertheless, our course team leader may still have to manage one major constraint: delays in completing writing and editing by staff members who are assigned part time to distance education programs. When they are unable to deliver materials on time, they cite heavy workloads in their home departments as an excuse. Sometimes the delays have stopped delivery of course materials; other times the course leader has had to change writers half way through production, which makes it difficult for the team to meet deadlines. I use my experience at the universities of Nairobi and Botswana as a context for the following description of events, especially regarding the use of learning technologies.

The team's planning and design stage begins with a situation analysis to determine learners' and the institution's needs before measuring these needs against available resources and operating constraints. It is critical to analyze all the needs, because many decisions are made concerning the rationale and viability of a course at this early stage. For example, when planning the distance-mode Diploma in Primary Education Program launched in December 2000, we began by analyzing learners' needs in terms of their demographic, social, and academic backgrounds before we compared the proposed syllabuses against these characteristics and our proposed media against the criteria of availability, accessibility, and affordability to both learners and teachers (Bates 1995). Our learners and teachers need to interact with learning technologies in a friendly atmosphere, but we must first determine which technologies are most easily accessible to them. For example, in a small survey for a program offered by the Centre for Continuing Education of the University of Botswana, we found that 33 of the 38 students had access to a radio and a cassette player, 27 to a videocassette player, 22 to television sets, and 20 to telephone lines, but fewer than five could easily access a computer. This minor survey showed that we could reach many students in a cost-effective manner if we used a combination of print plus radio and audiocassette technologies.

The geographical distribution of students helps us decide where to locate the study centers: where most of students live, the availability of tutors, and the location of physical facilities required for face-to-face tutorials. Sometimes we have used needs assessment reports completed by other groups; the Diploma in Primary Education at the University of Botswana, for example, was launched based on the results of a needs assessment survey commissioned by the Department of Teacher Training and Development in the Botswana Ministry of Education.

Following the needs assessment, our course team analyzes the syllabuses against learner characteristics and draws up program objectives and assessment mechanisms, and determines how and which learner support strategies will work given the geographical distribution of students.

Finally, they plan a budget and identify possible sites for learner support services. Usually our course team consists of subject/course content coordinators (the team leaders), academic authors, a distance education specialist, a graphic designer, an editor, a media officer, a learner support specialist, and a representative from Library Services. In most instances, course coordinators are full-time faculty members from the Distance Education unit with responsibilities for the different academic programs. Currently, we have subject/course coordinators for humanities, education, science, and social science; others will be recruited as the need arises. The team analyzes the syllabuses, identifies and fills any gaps, and develops course objectives and outlines. The course objectives clearly state the desired performance outcomes. The course outlines show the content topics and the component parts of each module. At this stage, we also design the teaching and learning strategy. For example, each module is divided into a maximum of 15 units or chapters. Thus when the University converts other programs to the semester system, distance education students can be advised to study one unit per week in a 15-week semester. We also design the assessment strategy so that assessment for each module is by two written assignments: one timed or supervised test and a final examination. Writers are advised to generate test questions as they write the course materials. Developing interactive study materials is a major priority for us, so the print-based materials contain questions, learning objectives, summaries, and other activities designed to engage students in active thinking during the course. Assessment strategies are designed to facilitate regular written feedback between learners and course tutors. I find that asking learners to write two take-home assignments and one timed examination tells me how well they have read and understood the course materials. Generally, our course materials gain credibility by being written and reviewed by academic staff who teach at that level in face-to-face programs. Although pilot testing is ideal, it has not been possible for many institutions to test materials with students before publication because of constraints of time and money. However, after a course is distributed, the editor and subject coordinators keep logbooks where they record corrections from students and tutors for use when the course is revised.

The functions of the audiocassette as a learning technology are to supplement the print materials, provide summaries, clarify certain concepts that the students may find difficult to understand, develop pronunciation in languages, teach some practical aspects of music that require sound, facilitate discussions during students' self-help study groups, facilitate learning any time anywhere (as long as the learner has a cassette player), and reduce feelings of isolation: the voice on the tape belongs to the person the student met during the face-to-face tutorials. According to Kabonoki, students like the audio programs because

> Voices are clear ... it made things clear which I could not understand by just reading ... I could associate the information in the print module with what I heard on the cassette ... [it] helped me with assignments ... they are easy to follow ... they introduce the lesson ... they act as reminder for my reading ... if you do not get things clear, you revert to the cassette.
>
> (2000: 5)

However, our students also ask us to test all dubbed cassette tapes to avoid distributing blanks, to reduce the information load, and to label each cassette clearly.

Development and production of audiocassette tapes starts at the course planning and design stage. When analyzing the syllabuses, writers are shown the entire media mix, told that print is the main medium, and introduced to the functions of audio. After writing the print materials, writers are then trained to write "for the ear" before writing, editing, and recording the scripts in the studios. The scripts are of broadcast quality, but we do not go on air for fear our learners who work during the day may not be able to hear the broadcasts: audiocassette tapes are much more flexible for our learners.

Learner support services

In Kenya and Botswana, these support services take the form of tutorials during school vacations when tutors and facilities are available. These support services also link to other educational institutions to maximize the use of resources. The first tutorial session, held soon after registration, introduces students to the course materials, the distance mode of study, and use of the library. Students are told about assessment procedures, assignments, due dates, and the schedule for supervised tests and examinations. The second session is held after students have submitted their coursework for marking. They receive feedback on their performance on assignments, are encouraged to discuss difficult content areas, and write supervised or timed tests. In the final tutorial session, students discuss course materials with their tutors and each other before writing the end-of-module examination. Each tutorial session lasts 7 to 10 days depending on the number of courses per academic program. Each course is allocated four hours per tutorial session in addition to library and private study time.

Tutors are chosen according to the academic qualifications required. Before tutorials begin, the tutors are taught to promote learner-sensitive advising, tutoring, and assessing academic progress. Despite this training, some tutors still prefer traditional "telling" methods and pay little attention to the designed learning process embedded in the course materials. These tutors are often heard to say that the time allocated for face-to-face tutorials is not adequate to cover a module of 12 to 15 chapters. Clearly they have not grasped the distance-mode concept that the course materials carry the primary teaching function and that their own role is to facilitate rather than transmit, that is, to help learners with difficult new concepts they encounter in their study materials.

Our students value the face-to-face tutorials for the personal, real-time interaction with tutors and fellow students, and they often demand more face-to-face contact with their tutors. For example, after the first residential session on the Diploma in Primary Education (DPE) Program at the University of Botswana, students were heard to say:

> I feel quite great that I am one of those chosen to undergo this training program ... I have learnt many methods ... the orientation was good. There are however certain areas where we can improve ... instead of queuing for study materials ... these can be given during tutorials ... I feel so great you know ... every time I open my modules and see "University of Botswana" ... I see myself as a full-time learner here ... I am highly delighted because I had never thought of entering "University of Botswana" ... but with the DPE, it has been possible.
>
> (University of Botswana 2000)

We collect feedback on our course materials and the success or failure of tutorials by administering questionnaires to both students and tutors at the end of each tutorial session. This enables the University of Botswana to assess whether tutors were prepared and whether students had read their modules before the residential session. One result from these evaluation exercises that concurs with my experiences at the University of Nairobi is that students prefer to be "taught" rather than actively study the course modules.

The library service is vital because in our courses we ask students to borrow books that contain additional information not found in our own course materials. The libraries also afford the students a quiet place to read during tutorial sessions. After the tutorial session, students are encouraged to use library facilities near their homes where additional reference materials have been placed. To strengthen the library services for distant learners, the University of Botswana and the University of Nairobi have forged collaborative links with other educational institutions such as colleges of education and other community service institutions. I have also been able to place book boxes for use by distant learners in institutions outside the national library service.

Key advice to others

Based on my own experience, I provide the following points as guides to others who may find themselves faced with similar concerns:

1 Faculty are key to the program's success. Try to ensure stable arrangements that provide adequate time and payment.
2 Monitor the technology infrastructure and student access so that other technologies can be added as they become available.
3 Do a careful needs analysis and be aware of the work of others that you can use to enhance your understanding of students' needs.
4 Provide training for faculty, writers, designers, and tutors.
5 Promote active learning to reduce student dropout.
6 Monitor students' satisfaction and learning.
7 Keep track of needed changes for eventual program redevelopment.
8 Encourage students to develop personal responsibility for learning.
9 The tutor is the program's face and voice. Be sure that tutors receive sufficient training and support to ensure they support the program's values.

Conclusion

Clearly the introduction of any new learning technology needs careful planning, and the sustained use of all learning technologies requires adequate infrastructure, responsive learner services, and integrated policies. Various operational factors constrain my practice in a context of larger issues: the lack of consistent resources, both material and human, and some inappropriate administrative systems. Yet despite these barriers and frustrations, we in Africa have made considerable progress and will endeavor to continue to do so, for this is our future.

References

Bates, A.W. (1995) *Technology, Open Learning and Distance Education.* London: Routledge.

Dodds, T., Nonyongo, E., and Glennie, J. (1999) "Co-operation, Competition or Dominance: A Challenge in Southern Africa," in K. Harry (ed.) *Higher Education Through Open and Distance Learning.* London: Routledge.

Kabonoki, K. (1999) "Building Quality in Media Materials for Distance Learning," L. Greying and M. Andrew, Allenby In-Home Power Learning, South Africa (eds) *OLISA Review* 5.

Kabonoki, K. (2000) "A Starting Point in the Use of Technology for Distance Learning: University of Botswana Experience." Paper presented at the 2nd National Distance Education Association of South Africa (NADEOSA), Pretoria: August.

Kamau, J.W. (1997) "The External Degree Programme, University of Nairobi: Case Study," in Commonwealth of Learning (ed.) *Quality Assurance Training Tool Kit.* Vancouver: Commonwealth of Learning.

Maskow, M. (2001) "Radio as a Learning Technology," in E.J. Burge (ed.) *The Strategic Use of Learning Technologies, New Directions for Adult and Continuing Education No. 88.* San Francisco, CA: Jossey-Bass.

Mphinyane, O.P. (1993) "Distance Education in Botswana: Its Present and Potential Role in Human Resource Development." Unpublished master's thesis, University of London, Institute of Education.

Odumbe, J.O. (1998) "University of Nairobi: Distance Education Teachers' Programme," in Commonwealth of Learning (ed.) *Learners Support System Training Tool Kit.* Vancouver: Commonwealth of Learning.

O'Rourke, J. (2001) "Print," in E.J. Burge (ed.) *The Strategic Use of Learning Technologies, New Directions for Adult and Continuing Education No. 88.* San Francisco, CA: Jossey-Bass.

Perraton, H. (1993) "National Developments and International Co-operation in Distance Education in Commonwealth Africa," in K. Harry, M. John, and D. Keegan (eds) *Distance Education: International Perspectives.* London, Routledge.

Southern African Development Community (SADC) (1998) "Transport and Commonwealth Report." Maputo: SADC.

University of Botswana (2000) "The Distance Educator." A Newsletter of the Distance Education Unit. Gaborone: University of Botswana, Centre for Continuing Education.

Uys, P. (1999) "University of Botswana: Strategic Educational Technology Plan." Report submitted to the University of Botswana, Gaborone, Botswana.

Part 3

Practice issues

Catherine Cavanaugh, Evelyn Ellerman, Lori Oddson, and Arlene Young use their own experience as teachers and student support facilitators to explore their ambivalent and sometimes conflicting reactions toward electronic communications technologies. Issues of interaction, autonomy, and access are predominant in their discussions of the cyberclassroom. Gill Kirkup uses her puzzlement about a photograph on the class Web site to explore issues of identity representation, gender presentation, and adult learning. Both Suzanne Sexty and Lantana Usman examine particular technologies. Suzanne Sexty explores the design and usability issues surrounding the collaborative development of a library Web site on information research skills for adult learners. Lantana Usman critiques the provision of radio programs for nomadic Nigerian women and recommends that the women be actively involved in program policy development if the programs are to be relevant to their life conditions and learning needs. Edith Mhehe also addresses issues of policy. Concerned at the lack of women registrants at the Open University of Tanzania, she illustrates how policy and practice converge to frustrate the women's ability to study successfully and recommends institutional strategies for alleviating these difficulties.

6 Lessons from our cyberclassroom

Catherine Cavanaugh, Evelyn Ellerman, Lori Oddson, and Arlene Young

Introduction

We welcomed the invitation to contribute to this book as an opportunity to reflect more systematically on a subject that is making a significant impact on our work and teaching practice. We were asked to focus on technology and learners' concerns in postsecondary education. For us these days, this primarily means digital communications and computer-mediated teaching-learning. What follows is an extension of conversations we have had among ourselves and with other colleagues.

To prepare this chapter we met face to face on three occasions. After Candas and Timothy, our facilitators and editors, recorded and transcribed our discussion, we used e-mail and file-sharing to refine their notes and comment on one another's work. Each of us worked on that section of the manuscript that reflected her primary interests and concerns. This way of working meant that we used the technology that we analyzed and in some important ways mirrored the process by which we increasingly interact with students.

Context and assumptions

Athabasca University (AU), Alberta, is an open and distance education institution in Canada (http://www.athabscau.ca). Its mandate has been to remove the barriers that restrict entry to and success in university-level studies and to increase access and success for all marginalized groups in society. The university's current *Strategic University Plan* anticipates positioning the institution now as a "virtual campus/electronic university." The expectation is that over time our print-based courses will increasingly adopt curricula that depend to a large extent upon the use of digital communication systems. Experimentation with online courses, desktop videoconferencing, and computer-mediated learning has thus begun in earnest.

Because AU is expanding its use of digital communications technology, we wish to use this chapter to focus on what we see as the gap between the promise of the technology and our experiences with it; our shifting role as teachers in a computer-mediated learning environment; and the impact of computer technologies on working conditions and on our students.

We began by discussing our experiences (and frustrations) with the technology, but quickly realized that we needed to pause and examine our fundamental understanding about teaching and learning. For example, if we view teaching as primarily a process of inputting information, then technology that enhances our ability to do this will be viewed as a good thing. On the other hand, if we believe personal interactions and relationships are paramount in a learning process, then we will approach the technology selectively to ensure the results we need.

Cathy was concerned that we are introducing new technologies into existing hierarchical structures. She reminded us that historically the introduction of new technologies has tended to reinforce rather than disrupt existing power relationships. In women's studies, her objective is to " 'teach for change' in ways that generate new ideas and stimulate individuals to think about questions in new ways." For this reason, she said, "we need to question whether the adoption of a particular technology will help or promote change."

Lori's experience of working with hundreds of instructors who have taught courses using self-instructional print materials has shown that there is more to the teaching process than simply facilitating the student's mastery of the "knowledge in the box." She worries that the pressure to digitize AU courses could diminish the energy that the institution directs toward disenfranchised student groups – or worse, that AU activity might serve a more narrowly defined student group: those who own and are comfortable using micro-computers.

As an open distance university, AU has always emphasized access and has responded to the rapidly changing learning environment. For example, early in the movement toward digitization, AU discussed how it could help students acquire and use computer technology. However, although digital access is now more affordable and reliable, we are concerned that the allure of new technology should not lead us to disregard the university's mission statement. Evelyn asks how we "justify the claim that we are an open university if we increasingly put the cost of a computer, modem, and Internet connection between our students and a university education."

Rather than replace the telephone as an important tool in distance education, staff at AU use computer applications that operate in conjunction with telephones, at least for students in North America. However, students are increasingly referred to information contained on AU's Web site. Furthermore, students living outside North America must rely solely on the Internet for communication and other purposes. In view of our institutional objective to make education accessible, we need to ask how these developments work to favor already privileged students over disadvantaged students. Thus efforts to provide students with access to computers through partnership arrangements (e.g., other educational institutions, public libraries, and the like) are important. So too is negotiating for lower prices for equipment and Internet service, as well as ensuring adequate technical support.

Because AU's success over 30 years has relied on its flexible delivery systems, we need to maintain this flexibility despite pressures to convert to a one-size-fits-all digital communication model. Beginning with the question "What is our objective?" reminds us of what is really only common sense: Technologies must be used where they seem most appropriate to the specific teaching-learning situation. Computer technology provides sophisticated tools we can use to accomplish the main objective, that is, making knowledge available at a distance. Nonetheless, each of us has our own stories about computer technology derailing us from that objective. It takes time to learn to use a computer effectively. Just "talking" across the university can require a wide range of protocols and frameworks that make the simplest tasks cumbersome and time-consuming. Athabasca University has yet to adopt standard teaching-learning software: students need Lotus Notes for some courses and a Web browser for others. New students can take a week or more to learn how to sign on to computer conferences. Our perception is that using computer technology seems to come more easily to students of the traditional university age, 18–24 years, from urban Canada, who used computers at school. Other students have acquired computer skills in their jobs. Of the remainder, many are motivated to learn because they fear being out of touch. To be successful computer users, however, they must have enough money to acquire the equipment and enough free time to adapt to what Evelyn describes as a "clunky system."

Computer technology can be made a little less clunky. We recognize that decisions about computer hardware and software are usually in the hands of those who manage the computing services department. We have a responsibility to influence their decision-making. We can recommend standard programs for communications, word-processing, and conferences, and make arrangements for students to purchase and upgrade programs at minimal cost and offer distance-delivered training programs. Most important is to make our needs as users known to the technical staff.

In search of magic

Computer technology affects the teaching-learning process in ways that seem contradictory – or at least paradoxical. For this reason, many academics are taking a critical perspective on its introduction. We appreciate its potential to democratize learning, its capacity to counter hegemonic knowledge production, but we are guarded about how it invisibly reshapes the context of knowledge production. We can recall the energy surge when students in a class or on the telephone connect ideas in a new way or make a wonderful discovery: the "Ah-ha!" experience. But Evelyn wonders: "Will the new technologies come between me and my students? I am not a facilitator; I am a teacher. I am in search of magic. I want wonder and magic, but I feel I am in a clunky environment."

At AU individual instructors in different disciplines approach the use of computer technology in various ways. For example, the women's studies program takes one approach, whereas the Master's in Distance Education (MDE) program takes another. In Cathy's view:

> The new technologies have a particular appeal for women's studies in that e-mail and other electronic tools allow students to connect and therefore learn from one another in ways that were not previously possible. At the same time, most Women's Studies students carry a double or triple load, with family and work obligations in addition to their studies. If the technology adds time to their work day they will (wisely) avoid it. They will only use it if it is a convenient and practical means of getting the job done.

Other difficulties arise: we have learned that adopting computer technology typically adds work for the instructor or tutor in an environment where cutbacks have already increased teaching workloads. For Cathy, this is a real dilemma. Increasingly students in her program are using e-mail as a primary means of communicating with their instructor or tutor: these students are, however, still a small minority. She feels it is important to encourage the use of the Internet if only to give students an opportunity to acquire or improve computer skills that are in high demand in the workplace. The program is incorporating computer technology, beginning with a Web page and links to supplementary resources. The next step will be to use a computer conference in one of the undergraduate courses. But each step will be evaluated in terms of student use, the effect on instructor or tutor workload, and the impact on the teaching-learning process.

The MDE program, on the other hand, makes extensive use of e-mail and computer conferencing. These activities, unlike independent study or classroom-based delivery, run 24 hours a day, 7 days a week, with the expectation that the instructor or tutor will be available daily rather than several times a week. Arlene instructs a course in the program and finds that monitoring computer conferences is time-consuming, and this fact is not always accounted for in workloads. For students, however, computer conferences facilitate collaboration across time and distance in ways not contemplated until recently. Many students mention in their course evaluations that participating in computer conferences helped them to express their ideas, something they may feel constrained from doing in a traditional classroom. Evelyn adds that asynchronous conferencing "gives students the chance to edit, to be thoughtful."

Cathy raised the issue of the supposed neutrality of the new technology:

We work in a hierarchical institution. When you add the impact of new technologies, these hierarchies are further obscured by the assumption that the technologies are neutral. In working with computers in particular, but also other technologies such as the telephone, as an instructor within our system I feel I have a power advantage.

An important issue, therefore, is how we adopt computer technology so as to disrupt existing power relationships by enabling students to engage in their learning process and generate new understanding.

When we use computer technology, we influence how we interact with each other. E-mail is an efficient way to make contact because it is asynchronous, but it can also be impersonal. It allows students to conduct academic and administrative tasks at their convenience, but it can result in expectations of an almost instant response. Indeed, in responding to increased student expectations, AU has established turnaround timelines for replying to students. Another concern is the typical terseness of e-mail. As Cathy says, "I think of it as requiring an instant, brief response, unlike telephone tutoring, which is very personal, intimate almost." At the same time, we recognize that adding e-mail to the communications mix allows students to choose a level of interaction and intimacy. Some will choose e-mail, possibly because it is efficient or less personal, whereas others will choose the telephone. Institutions should ensure that students continue to be able to select from various communication modes that are relevant to their learning styles and objectives.

Democratizing the virtual classroom

Historically, AU has seen itself as a learner-centered institution. In the AU model of distance education, the teaching function is distributed among the course package, the writer, professor, instructor or tutor, and learner.

Over the years, the printed course package has become the primary teaching tool at AU. Considerable attention, therefore, has focused on the design and delivery quality of the course package. So precisely developed was this Fordist model of educational delivery that much of the actual task of teaching continues to be delegated to part-time, contract tutors, whereas designing and upgrading the course package is left to a much smaller group of full-time professors or academic coordinators. This course development and delivery model contributed to an internal institutional myth that at AU the learning environment is nonhierarchical, or at least more egalitarian than the traditional university classroom. The university's mission statement – to provide open access in a flexible and appropriate manner – reinforces this notion that somehow we are already teaching in the most democratic way possible. But these and other practices also obscure the reality that the professor has designed and perhaps written the course, designed or approved the method of evaluation, chosen the readings, and hired the tutor; and that the tutor and professor both evaluate, teach, and grade, leaving the learner fewer choices than a democratic model might suggest.

The advent of electronic technologies, particularly the Internet, has challenged the faculty in ways that have surprised and even shocked many of us. As Evelyn said:

> It is as if I were watching myself in a mirror. Right now, I am exploring a very tight circle of knowledge production between instructor, learner, and technology rather than the usual assumption that the technology is a minimal factor and that the circle is really composed of instructor, learner, and course material. This is probably because I still experience the technology as opaque rather than transparent. This often is not necessarily the case with my students, many of whom are in their 20s and 30s and work in the communications business. They are teaching *me* how to teach in this new environment.

But they can be less critical of the technology and its pedagogical implications.

We are skeptical about the claim that these media necessarily present a radical democratization of learning. "In women's studies," Cathy remarked, "I hope to challenge my students to think about questions in new ways. My primary question is, how can I use this particular technology to promote change?" The group agreed that our teaching comes with ideological and generational "wrappings" and that these are not only evident in our course materials, but also in our approach to the new technologies.

We discussed how the electronic environment polarizes notions of the respective roles of student and instructor. Evelyn said:

> In a sense, the new technologies have magnified the rhetoric of educational philosophy over the last 30 years – the notion that we help students acquire skills, not content; that teacher education must therefore focus on process. This trend has serious implications for maintaining cultural literacy and for redefining notions of leadership and responsibility.

There are inherent paradoxes in the electronic technologies themselves: They have the potential to be democratizing, but in practice are often conservative, hierarchical, and therefore undemocratic. The logic traditionally used to program computers is hierarchical and linear. Most commercial CD-ROMs and computing software packages operate at best as gathering and sorting devices that offer a limited number of response choices for users. And most of these programs replicate Eurocentric, patriarchal paradigms in the international language of power: English. As course designers, we might want to overcome some of these undemocratic features by constructing our own electronic learning resources, but this goal is largely out of reach because of cost. In fact, like most universities we have barely enough resources to institute, let alone maintain, the shift to electronic technologies. This puts all of us at further risk of influence and coercion by government and corporate funding sources. Despite these important concerns, our group accepts the democratizing *potential* of these technologies. For example, Cathy believed that the technologies could offer women "radical possibilities for intellectual exchange outside traditional classrooms and (importantly) strict disciplinary boundaries."

In the end we felt alternately engaged and frustrated by the issue of democratizing the cyberclassroom. Our reactions seem to stem primarily from having to engage both the existing mythologies of distance education and the emerging mythologies of electronic communication. We believe that the new technologies have disrupted the familiar dynamic tensions between technology and education. As a result, we must now do a great deal more than simply investigate electronic technologies as "just one more teaching tool." The new environment affects us at every level of our working lives, and we wonder if we have the time or the energy to deal with it.

Conclusion

In many ways, computer technology appears to be a boon to distance education. This is especially true at AU, where our stated mission is to remove barriers to postsecondary education. Computer technology appears to enhance access, making university education available to all regardless of geographic location. Moreover, connecting individual learners through the Internet promises a radically new learning environment. In the borderless environment of cyberspace, there is no *in* or *out*, and every voice is authorized to speak. For those of us committed to emancipatory education and community-based learning, the new technologies hold particular appeal.

However, each of us takes a measured approach to computer-mediated learning. We are signing on to the cyberclassroom, but it seems that the technology itself makes us hyperaware of the teaching-learning environment. Like Evelyn, we are "in an experimental mode in learning to apply the new technologies, wanting to explore them but also maintaining a critical perspective ... It's a tentative process," she explained, "I'm taking a few steps at a time."

In part, our caution reflects our own level of skill and (un)familiarity with the new technologies. We all regularly use computer technology, but too often we experience it as hampering rather than facilitating communication. With practice and use, what seems to happen at best is that the technology becomes de-mechanized and can promote flexibility.

We were all trained in traditional classrooms and are attempting to translate that experience into a computerized environment. So far, our experiments and investigations are halting. Does this reflect our inexperience and lack of skills, or is there a deeper concern about how the new technologies alter our relationships to knowledge production? Are we, as Evelyn implied, being

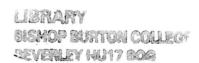

turned into facilitators and our students into information gatherers? Can the current rush to adopt computer technologies be divorced from the material conditions in which we teach and learn?

The introduction of computer technologies and the associated political and economic assumptions have introduced a number of work-related concerns for us: first is a significantly greater workload and work speed-ups; second is the imposition of evaluation policies that privilege certain quantifiable outcomes (e.g., the number of graduates) over the learning process; third is the impact of technology on the dynamic relationship between the teacher and student; and fourth is the assumption that we can manage a computerized environment. This assumption may be an illusion. At one level, we ask which technologies are best suited to our pedagogical and intellectual purposes, but there is the larger question of the imperatives of the technology itself and how these shape what we do, how we think about ourselves, and what we know. Perhaps, as Evelyn pointed out, part of the problem is that there just is no good fit between the ways we think about ourselves, the technology we use, and the environment in which we work. "There is a 'nowness' about new technology that is seductive. We think that we really ought to be using it but this nowness also works to make us forget what came before." This loss of context can cut us off from asking important questions about our relationship to the technology and its potential as a learning and teaching tool.

Each of us works in a period of transition. Our own strategies have centered on reading widely, watching what others are doing, discussing with peers their experience, developing awareness of our own and our students' level of comfort with computer technology, and experimenting and assessing the results.

Effective use of the technology requires that we ask initial and ongoing questions about any new technology (*it*) such as: Who has it? Who can get it? Who has the skills to make it work? How much monitoring is necessary to assure a positive experience with it? What is being done in the application of the technology to make sure it works? How are programs interconnected in their use of it or by their use of it? Do students become better critical thinkers or writers by using it? Do they hear their own voice better when they use it? Is there a risk that it will get out of hand?

The answers to these questions will depend on various factors including the needs of students, ideas about what education is or should be, specific program needs and disciplinary interests, individual learning needs and abilities, institutional mythologies, economic and political constraints, and political and social climates. As the process of finding answers continues, so will the discovery of new questions.

Recommendations

We reject the business model of education (students are customers and teachers are knowledge workers) and we support a collaborative model where students and instructors produce knowledge and seek change interactively and democratically. These values and our practical experience led us to develop recommendations that address global rather than specific issues centered on the cyberclassroom. To stimulate your thinking, we express them as a series of questions.

For institutions

1   Have you *reflected on your primary principles*, including identifying student needs? Have you established what you hope to accomplish using computer technology? Are roles and responsibilities clearly delineated?
2   Have you *researched course and program delivery strategies* to determine their suitability for the subject matter and identifiable learners' needs?
3   Have you *collaborated with stakeholders* to ensure their meaningful participation in the planning, implementation, and evaluation stages?
4   Have you *developed open-ended feedback mechanisms* so that the information collected can be used to refine or improve systems?
5   Have you *committed institutional resources* (time and money) necessary to train instructors and support students in their use of computer technology? How best can you analyze infrastructure and sustainability issues?

For instructors, teachers, and tutors

1   Are you *prepared for uncertainty*? In some cases, students will be experienced with the technology and you will learn from them. In other cases, you will need to deal with reluctance and inexperience.
2   Are you *willing to experiment*, experience, stumble, and rejoice at the evolving and iterative process?
3   Do you *share experiences* with other instructors and collaborate in the development of guidelines for those who are just beginning to use the technology?
4   Do you *ensure that students understand the environment* in which they are learning and what is expected of them (e.g., apply critical analysis to information from the Internet)?
5   Do you *evaluate practices* by providing meaningful feedback to your institution?

For students

1   Have you *assessed the skills and abilities* that you bring to the educational process?
2   Have you *conveyed your needs* to your instructors and learned how to negotiate institutional requirements?

3   Have you *accepted your own strengths and weaknesses* and recognized the dynamic environment in which you find yourself?

4   Do you *participate and communicate fully* in the learning process?

5   Will you *critically reflect on your educational experience* and share your evaluation with instructors and the institution(s) involved?

Acknowledgment

We thank Candas Jane Dorsey and Timothy Anderson for their editorial assistance in stitching our pieces into whole cloth while respecting the unique texture of each.

Bibliography

Bender, G. and Druckrey, T. (eds) (1994) *Culture on the Brink: Ideologies of Technology*. Seattle, WA: Bay Press.

Burbules, N.C. and Callister, T.A. (2000) "Universities in Transition: The Promise and the Challenge of New Technologies," *Teachers College Record*, 102, 271–293.

Daniel, J.S. (1997) "Why Universities Need Technology Strategies," *Change*, 29 (July/August), 10–23.

Hanna, D.E. (1998) "Higher Education – In an Era of Digital Competition: Emerging Organizational Models," *Journal of Asynchronous Learning Networks*, 2, 1, 66–95.

Hawthorne, S. and Klein, R. (eds) (1999) *Cyberfeminism: Connectivity, Critique and Creativity*. North Melbourne: Spinifex Press.

Hopkins, P.D. (1998) *Sex/Machine: Readings in Culture, Gender, and Technology*. Bloomington, IN: Indiana University Press.

James, W.B. and Gardner, D.L. (1995) *Learning Styles: Implications for Distance Learning. New Directions for Adult and Continuing Education No. 67*. San Francisco, CA: Jossey-Bass.

Kent, T.W. and McNergney, R.F. (1999) *Will Technology Really Change Education? From Blackboard to Web*. Thousand Oaks, CA: Corwen Press.

Kirkup, G., Janes, K., Woodward, K., and Hovenden, F. (2000) *The Gendered Cyborg: A Reader*. London: Routledge in association with the Open University.

Massey, W.F. (1997) "Life on the Wired Campus: How Information Technology Will Shape Institutional Futures," in D.G. Oblinger and S.C. Rush (eds) *The Learning Revolution: The Challenge of Information Technology in the Academy*. Bolton, NY: Anker.

Miller, L. (1995) "Women and Children First: Gender and the Settling of the Electronic Frontier," in J. Brook and I.A. Boal (eds) *Resisting the Virtual Life: The Culture and Politics of Information*. San Francisco, CA: City Lights.

Mills, R. and Tait, A. (1996) *Supporting the Learner in Open and Distance Learning*. London: Pitman.

Phillips, M. and Kelly, P. (2001) "Learning Technologies for Learner Services," in E.J. Burge (ed.) *The Strategic Use of Learning Technologies, New Directions for Adult and Continuing Education No. 88*. San Francisco, CA: Jossey-Bass.

Plant, S. (1997) *Zeros and Ones: The Matrix of Women and Machines*. New York: Doubleday.

Simon Fraser University Telelearning Policy Initiative, and TeleEducationNB (1998) *Technology-Mediated Learning: Current Initiatives and Implications for Higher Education*. Online. Available: http://www.sfu.ca/tpi/cmec.htm.

7 Teacher or avatar? Identity issues in computer-mediated contexts

Gill Kirkup

> I was thinking that we all learn by experience, but some of us have to go to summer school.
>
> (De Vries 1965: 14)

The summer of 1983 was an exciting time for those of us working in women's studies at the Open University in the United Kingdom (OUUK). For nearly five years we campaigned for, designed, and finally produced the first under-graduate open and distance learning course in women's studies, which could be studied by anyone anywhere in the UK. For six weeks during July and August, over 600 students (90 percent women and 10 percent men) came, for a week each, to the campus of the University of East Anglia for the intensive residential component of the course. An OUUK women's studies summer school ran every summer from then until 1999. In 1999 the final cohort – just over 200 students – studied, argued, and enjoyed themselves; and in a different political and educational world, the undergraduate course, and with it the summer school, came to the end of its life.

In 1983 colleagues teaching women's studies in face-to-face contexts had been dubious about whether the self-reflective, personal-change aspects of women's studies, which were so much a part of its particular nature and its political project, could be reproduced without the intensive small-group experience. The OUUK course team wished to incorporate this intensive experience into the multiple-media structure of the OUUK's supported open and distance learning system. The summer residential school was designed as a distinct but integrated component of a course that used broadcast television and radio, audiotape, and interactive study texts, supported by optional small-group tutorials in local centers. In 1983 many OUUK courses used residential schools to give specific types of experience that could not be reproduced adequately through other media: for example, laboratory work, computer access, field work, or simulation. The Freirian (Freire 1990) objective of "liberatory" education through a group learning experience or, in 1970s feminist terms consciousness raising, was not the usual rationale for residential components of courses. But students brought to our residential school the immense wealth of their lived experience and used it collectively to reflect on the theories they were studying, as well as using those theories to reflect on their lived experience. They expected their teachers to engage in, if not lead, both activities. Students called this process "making sense of it," "finding the language to describe what I've always felt," and "finding other people who feel like me." There was a sense of discovering knowledge about gender from within oneself and through honest and authentic shared experience with others. There was a notion, criticized during the 1990s, of a real *I*, an authentic self, an identity that could be discovered, explored, and developed.

I remember the first week of that first year: the excitement of meeting in the flesh the students who had been composite abstractions in our heads for so long. Most of the teaching staff were part of the team who had designed and written the course, but they had had no direct contact with the students who, scattered all over the UK, were supported by local tutors who worked with them in their local area. The staff were excited; the students were excited. We wanted to see who our students were; they wanted to see what kind of people feminist academics were and maybe meet the authors of their study materials. Our appearance and behavior were taken as important symbols of the nature of women's studies in particular and feminism more widely. Staff represented feminist scholarship and feminist lived practice both to women's studies students and to students in other courses who were on campus at the same time. As well as socializing and having a sense of humor, we had to demonstrate *erudition* (to show that women's studies was properly scholarly). We embodied not only our *authentic* selves but also our *discipline*. Small issues such as the fact that many staff painted their toenails in the summer were seen as bodily signs that studying gender did not produce nonsexual women. As practitioners, we embodied our knowledge and skills, sometimes to the detriment as well as the benefit of those learning from us.

A colleague wrote recently:

> In higher education, our attention is expected to focus on the substance and complexities of the discipline and topic under discussion, not on our selves, our own interests or even on our personal reactions to the topic. Academic objectivity requires us to sift very carefully questions of true and false, right and wrong, valid or invalid, good and bad, insightful or obtuse from those of personal taste or distaste, political or religious commitment, fear or loathing, enthusiasm or delight. The pursuit of objectivity and the mistrust of the personal and private is the platonic moral heritage of all higher learning in the Western world.
>
> (Blake 2000: 187)

I suspect Blake would think that our women's studies residential schools transgressed in all the ways he listed. But feminism had declared that "the personal is political" and that the boundaries between public and private are political constructions that consign some people to the realms of the private and personal only, leaving them no place as social actors or in the construction of knowledge. One of the many aims of women's studies, along with its traditional scholarly aims such as developing analytical tools and critiquing bias in earlier theories of gender difference, is to validate personal experience as *real* knowledge and as a resource for testing theory. This method of learning, as well as constructing knowledge, corresponds well with the terminology of reflective practice and communities of practice (Schön 1983; Lave 1988; Lave and Wenger 1991), which also presume embodied actors.

Since the early 1980s, open and distance learning has expanded dramatically (in new incarnations such as "flexible and distributed learning") using new information and communication technologies (ICTs). This development has been accompanied by changes in the curriculum and in many countries in the organization of postschool education. At the same time, postmodernism produced a different understanding of identity as fractured and often internally contradictory. It has questioned the possibility of an authentic *I*, and the Internet, it has been argued, allows us to adopt any identity we choose for the time we are online (Turkle 1997). It is assumed to be the perfect environment for us to explore our many identities.

Yet as educators, we remain committed to the importance of integrating students as whole persons into the educational experience, helping them to become "deep" and reflective learners, knowing that all knowledge is situated knowledge (Haraway 1988; Harding 1993). We also develop ourselves as practitioners in a changing technological and ideological environment. Since that first women's studies course in 1983, I have tutored in a number of OUUK courses in various disciplines and year by year expanded my experience of using ICTs. In each teaching situation, an important issue is the context and identities of my students and myself and how we embody these identities in our use of ICTs. In any distributed or distance education system, the identities of both students and teachers must be represented somehow and articulated into a learning community. But how do we represent and articulate if our identities are always unfixed?

In this chapter, therefore, I reflect on issues such as *situatedness*, identity, authenticity, and embodiment as they have presented themselves to me as I used computer-mediated learning. Is my identity as a teacher an aspect of an authentic *me* to which I have a duty (to myself and others in contact with this aspect of me) to make coherent and to keep grounded in lived experience? Or is my identity as a teacher, and in particular as an online teacher, a performance constructed for a particular moment with reference to little else? How do I represent or create my identity as an online teacher? Do I represent my material self with biographical text and images, or do I create symbolic *avatars* that exist only in the online teaching-learning environment, embodying only the identity of me as the online teacher? An avatar is a graphical icon that represents a material person or an aspect of his or her identity in a computer-based system. Avatars can be found in various chat domains and other multiuser domains. In sophisticated forms they can be animated and programmed to interact with other avatars.

Where are you?

A common experience of anyone joining online forums is that one of the first questions they are asked is "Where are you from?" followed by some other personal questions about age or sex perhaps. This curiosity always seems to me to strike a jarring note because one of the promoted advantages of the Internet is that it transcends distance and allows one to talk to anyone in the world as if they were online in the next room. The language of the Internet suggests that once online, we enter a virtual place (the Net) that transcends the material location of our keyboarding bodies. But that first question – "Where are you from?" – establishes the notion of geographical distance and also of real embodiment, connected via the technology to others also embodied in material geographic settings. Despite all the cyber-real rhetoric, as social beings we need to locate people relative to ourselves – in space and with respect to other criteria that are important to us – effectively to embody them in the technology. This locating action is especially true if we are engaged in an educational activity with other people. If we fail to acknowledge the constraints of the material context and real lives of our students and ourselves, ICT-based education can become an unsatisfactory experience.

This need for embodiment seems to be implicitly accepted by online teachers at one level even when the rhetoric refers to disembodiment. In setting up any online seminar when participants have never met in the flesh, teachers are advised to encourage students or participants to introduce themselves personally, perhaps including a photo image or representative icon. The presumption is that what participants say will be selective but "truthful": it will reflect the material reality of their lives rather than a constructed virtual identity. Why should this construction be so? Would the kind of learning that takes place in the group be invalid if instead of short autobiographical statements with a photo participants created a virtual identity represented by an avatar? And how should we as teachers present ourselves? We have usually made more demands on students for self-exposure than we have on ourselves. We are the students' teachers, not necessarily their friends. Are we exempt from identity selection issues?

Who are you?

In one of the first courses I tutored via the Web, one of the first of the students' actions was to circulate photographs of themselves, some with a little quiz such as a group photograph and a request that the other members of the group guess who in the group was the student. I refused to provide a picture. I was unconvinced that it was necessary, and like many academics I have more confidence in my textual identity than in my physical visual identity. In this course, unlike the women's studies course where my physical identity gave me authority in the content, this was a postgraduate professional teaching course, and I did not think I looked like a professional teacher. I decided to present myself only through textual means. I had no idea until much later of the mystery that my action produced for the students, even long after the course finished. Students from this course who visit me at work have commented that I do not appear as they imagined me, or they comment on the degree of consonance between my textual identity and my bodily image. They have also told me about the e-mails that they exchanged with each other while they tried to guess how I looked and develop a composite image that for them literally embodied my identity.

This year, for a different course I tutor online, I removed the identity issue by putting in a small photograph of myself and a short biography. No student has commented on it. I have to admit that I spent longer deciding which photo I wished to use than I would spend deciding how to dress for the first face-to-face tutorial I might have with a group of students! The problem with photographs is that they are limited images of embodiment. When we meet people in the flesh, the image we present is composed not only of how we look but also how we sound, how we animate our bodies, even how we smell. So much is missing from a photograph that the deliberate choice of a fantasy avatar might in some ways represent symbolically more about ourselves than just a picture. I have had a similar problem with designing a personal Web page. As academics at the OU, we are expected to create a Web page that somehow, in one document with perhaps hypertext links, should represent the sum of what we are professionally to everyone who accesses it: students, colleagues, and strangers. No other document in my life tries to do this for all these audiences. Even CVs are tailored for particular purposes. For me, the problem of finding one visual image to represent me, or one Web text to do the job, illustrates the reality of the postmodern argument that identities are multiple, if not fractured. Even what appears to be a coherent identity, that of teacher, is a coherent integration of many identities. The limits of computer-mediated communication mean that only the most simplified identities can be adequately represented or performed by most people.

Is it me or is it the software?

Bill Gates had a vision of the perfect online educational system and the perfect online teacher:

> When the information highway is in operation, the texts of millions of books will be available. A reader will be able to ask questions, print the text, read it on screen, or even have it read in his choice of voices. He'll be able to ask questions. It will be his tutor.

(1995: 195)

Here the perfect tutor is an intelligent machine; the problem of representing or embodying the human teacher is removed. My experience of online teaching indicates that what was required of me in some courses was equivalent in part to the attributes of a perfect machine, that is, to be always available when the students "needed" me, responsive to all individual queries, and responsible for the success of online group interactions. My sense of there being nowhere I could go to escape from the online demands of students can be compared with slavery or with the situation of a parent caring for an infant. My online teacher identity created a negative impact on my other identities, online and material. Here is an example. On one hot Sunday in June, I was in my campus office facilitating an online group of international students in a master's course. I felt none of the elation described by many teachers when they write about online teaching: the sense of breaking boundaries of time and space or communicating freely across the world. Instead I felt tired and exploited. I wanted to be with my family, who were enjoying a local festival; I wanted to be able to maintain reasonable boundaries between my work and my private time. I felt I could no longer control the various facets of my work or identity. There was no joy in this elision of work and leisure, in the dissolution of the boundary between my private time and my teaching time. Now, more than a year later, I am better able to impose order and control; I have built new boundaries to manage my professional and other identities.

Minds and bodies

I question the assumed value of ICTs for enabling the teacher and student to transcend the geographical and social barriers associated with time and distance and be able to engage in learning anywhere, any time, as anyone. It seems to me that nested in this notion of transcendence is the view that biological and social embodiment constrains rather than enriches (Tiffin and Rajasingham 1995).

If learners and teachers could transcend the limitations of being embodied, of being socially and economically situated (so many writers argue), we could get right down to the real educational business of dealing mind-to-mind with issues of the intellect. Drawing on my background in gender studies, I know that such a Platonic position is masculine. Historically, in Western and much Eastern culture the most highly valued knowledge has been that of highly abstract subjects such as philosophy, mathematics, and theology. These activities were considered best carried out by men, who denied their embodiment and lived where possible unpolluted by the nearness of the bodies and the demands of relationships with women and children. Our universities originally were places where celibate men studied, their monkishness a sign of their intellect: their focus on higher things. Others, most often women and young people, organized the physical necessities of material life for these men: preparing food, making clothes, and keeping the domestic and work environment clean and warm. Today knowledge-making is still a restricted privilege, and the restrictions apply in many forms. Who has the privilege now to engage in the abstract activity of knowledge creation – either online or on a university campus? Which identities are deemed to be appropriate for making knowledge?

Open and distance learning (ODL) was perhaps one of the first educational areas to situate students in the material world rather than remove them from it to a world of "dreaming spires," ivory towers, or green campuses. The ODL students have always been recognized as having primary identities outside their ODL course, and support for them was designed in part to help them manage all the conflicting demands of those identities. Research on female students in particular has argued that they have different material circumstances from men, different realities from which to draw for their intellectual scaffolding and their emotional and financial support (e.g., see Spronk's chapter in this book). In the 1980s and 1990s, female distance educators shared ideas and produced a range of papers on the issue of gender in ODL (Faith 1988; Burge and Lenskyj 1990; Kirkup 1996; Kirkup and von Prümmer 1990; Burge 1998). Books were written about the particular needs, motivations, and strengths of female ODL students (Lunneborg 1994; Heron 1997; von Prümmer 2000). This wealth of research has much to say about the opportunities and problems in acknowledging the diversity of students' embodied experiences.

Embodied experience is a key resource for using situated reasoning (Brown 1989) to make meaning for ourselves and for others. Bodies produce and locate knowledge and construct meanings. Gender is inscribed on our bodies (as are race and other important social differences). It is produced in the interactions our bodies have with others, and our bodies are for others always gendered signs. If we accept a definition of gender as a symbolic system indicating certain societal assumptions and expectations, it should not surprise us that technologies have gender or that our interaction with virtual bodies online corresponds to gender-related assumptions and expectations. Many people, in my experience, feel obvious discomfort in most online communications if they cannot ascribe gender to a participant. Although I draw here on a career of research on gender, the tools of gender analysis apply in other educational areas for revealing how other aspects of difference, diversity, and inequality operate.

Haraway (1996) argues that historically, not only attributes of gender, but of race, class, and language have defined who can validly know about the world. So instead of excluding some people from knowledge-making, our task now is to find ways of including a more diverse body of people. Doing so through an electronic medium will not necessarily make inclusion any easier than doing so in a face-to-face classroom. Brown wrote

> We all use our embodied and embedded position in the world to off-load onto our environment part of the representational and computational

burden of cognition. The processes that we use to do this allow us to respond in real time to events as they unfold in the world in which we are embedded.

(1989: 17)

Nowhere in Brown's (1989) work or writings by Lave and Wenger (1991) are political and social factors such as gender an explicit part of the debate. However, the logic of their argument is that these factors should be included, as should race and other important determinants of situatedness. Brown's hope for the creation of a "universal learning environment" would seem to be a contradictory hope if his learners are engaged in situated reasoning, as he calls it, or producing situated knowledge, as Haraway might describe it. Learners' embodiments will suggest different kinds of learning environments that allow people to choose to represent themselves differently and act out different identities. However, the presumption in this work is that any identity will have correspondence with the material world.

Authors such as Brown and Duguid reflect the focus on embodiment well when they identify education as a group process for constructing knowledge:

Together, members construct and negotiate a shared meaning, bringing the process of the group along collectively rather than individually. In the process, they become what the literary critic Stanley Fish [1980] calls a "community of interpretation" working towards a shared understanding of the matter under discussion.

(2000: 222)

A sense of community comes from a sense of shared identity, discourse, or values. These create a sense of trust between members of a community. In 1983 the OUUK's women's studies course created a "community of interpretation" that included women from across the UK. The face-to-face summer school was for many students the most exciting, and sometimes terrifying, catalyst in that interpretative process. We look now to reproduce the successful aspects of those summer schools using electronic means. But for this technology we have still to find our voices and our identities.

The Road goes ever on and on.

(Tolkien 1954: 48)

Because I am concerned about ICTs creating further educational inequalities, I have been struck by the truth of an argument by Brown and Duguid (2000) that our concern with the "information poor" having no access to education may be misplaced. It may be, they argue, that ICTs will provide the less wealthy with their only access to information. The rich, they argue, will be able to afford for themselves or their children the luxury of full-time study on conventional campuses where they will incorporate electronic and distributed learning as part of a rich, integrated educational experience. This experience will allow them also to develop and integrate their various identities to produce coherent and confident social actors. As an experienced ODL researcher, course designer, and teacher, my concern focuses on how we offer online experiences that achieve similar outcomes, rather than outcomes that offer only opportunities for the creation of constrained, simplistic identities and consequently constrained, simplistic knowledge production.

To produce coherent and confident social actors (i.e., learners and teachers) and skilled knowledge construction, we need a more complex understanding of how we represent, develop, and control the identities we produce online. As we become clearer about our online identities as teachers, and how we articulate these with our other identities and those of others, we will be better placed to help our students develop and manage their identities. This kind of help must be an important aspect of our online teaching. The concept of teacher-avatar could be very creative, but no teacher-avatar should ever float free from the material context in which the other aspects of that person are located – and nor should any student-avatar. Note here too that the technology in which these avatars exist should act only as the medium through which teaching-learning is carried on, not as the driver of the educational activities.

Our online identities and communities are not ways to transcend or ignore embodiment. Rather, they should be seen as technological contexts that allow us to explore and elaborate on our embodied selves and our embodied knowledge. We look for ways to explore and elaborate that are as challenging and exciting as those summer schools of the last century.

Guides to reflection

Working from my premise that situated knowledge generated in an online class should be an elaboration of our embodied selves, I propose the following questions.

1   Who are you in an online learning class? Who is (are) behind your photo? Reflect on the identity you think you portray.
2   Who do your students say you are? Does student feedback give you insights into other dimensions of a *you* they constructed?
3   What identities do students and the software impose on you as the instructor? Reconsider your response time to queries, the extent to which you intervene, when you decide to change topics, and how many topics can be engaged in at once, and students' reactions to these.
4   What about truth in advertising: are students who they say they are? How can we create a community of interpretation?
5   How can we ensure an authentic relationship between our online identities and our embodied keyboarding selves?

References

Blake N. (2000) "Tutors and Students without Faces or Places," *Journal of Philosophy of Education*, 34, 1, 183–197.

Brown, J.S. (1989) "Toward a New Epistemology for Learning," in C. Frasson and J. Gauthier (eds) *Intelligent Tutoring Systems at the Crossroad of AI and Education.* Norwood, NJ: Ablex.

Brown, J.S. and Duguid, P. (2000) *The Social Life of Information.* Boston, MA: Harvard Business School Press.

Burge, E.J. (1998) "Gender in Distance Education," in C.C. Gibson (ed.) *Distance Learners in Higher Education: Institutional Responses for Quality Outcomes.* Madison, WI: Atwood.

Burge, E.J. and Lenskyj, H. (1990) "Women Studying in Distance Education: Issues and Principles," *Journal of Distance Education*, 5, 1, 20–37.

De Vries, P. (1965) *The Tunnel of Love.* London: Penguin.

Faith, K. (ed.) (1988) *Toward New Horizons for Women in Distance Education.* London: Routledge

Freire, P. (1990) *Pedagogy of the Oppressed.* London: Penguin.

Gates, B. (1995) *The Road Ahead.* London: Penguin Viking.

Haraway, D.J. (1988) "Situated Knowledges: The Science Question in Feminism as a Site of Discourse on the Privilege of the Partial Perspective," *Feminist Studies*, 14, 3, 575–599.

Haraway, D.J. (1996) *Modest_Witness@Second_Millennium.FemaleMan_Meets_ OncoMouse.* London: Routledge.

Harding, S. (1993) "Rethinking Standpoint Epistemology: What is 'Strong Objectivity'?", in L. Alcoff and E. Potter (eds) *Feminist Epistemologies.* New York: Routledge.

Heron, M. (1997) *In My Own Skin: Dialogue with Women Students, Tutors and Counsellors. Researching Reality, Meaning, Change and Growth in the Open University.* Monograph. Walton Hall: Open University, Regional Academic Services.

Kirkup, G. (1996) "The Importance of Gender," in R. Mills and A. Tait (eds) *Supporting the Learner in Open and Distance Learning.* London: Pitman.

Kirkup, G. and von Prümmer, C. (1990) "Support and Connectedness: The Needs of Women Distance Education Students," *Journal of Distance Education*, 5, 2, 9–31.

Lave, J. (1988) *Cognition in Practice.* Boston, MA: Cambridge University Press.

Lave, J. and Wenger, E. (1991) *Situated Learning: Legitimate Peripheral Participation.* Boston, MA: Cambridge University Press.

Lunneborg, P.W. (1994) *OU Women: Undoing Educational Obstacles.* London: Cassell.

Schön, D. (1983) *The Reflective Practitioner.* New York: Basic Books.

Tiffin, J. and Rajasingham, L. (1995) *In Search of the Virtual Class. Education in an Information Society.* London: Routledge.

Tolkien, J.R.R. (1954) *Lord of the Rings* (2nd edn). London: Allen and Unwin.

Turkle, S. (1997) *Life on the Screen: Identity in the Age of the Internet.* New York: Touchstone Press.

von Prümmer, C. (2000) *Women in Distance Education.* London: Routledge.

8 Web-based research assistance

Suzanne Sexty

Introduction

Library support for distance learners is not a new phenomenon, and there are formal guidelines for providing such support (American Library Association 1998; Canadian Library Association n.d.). Although libraries have used various technologies, support has mainly been in the form of document delivery services. The reality is that libraries have not been able to offer distance learners the same research experiences as those enjoyed by learners who walk up to the reference desk in the library. Most distance learning courses were designed such that research materials were delivered to the learners rather than the learners searching for them. Because learners had limited, if any, access to library catalogues and indexes, it was deemed to be too difficult for them to do their own research, and courses were designed to eliminate the "problems" of research. Thus these courses also eliminated the opportunities for many valuable learning experiences. But this situation has now changed.

Change is familiar to librarians. When I entered the profession, my first job was to type the 3" × 5" cards for the card catalogue. In Canada few libraries now use a card catalogue, and fewer learners still use a typewriter. In more than 30 years working in all types of libraries and at various levels of responsibility, I have been guided not by the differences in my jobs, nor by how new technologies have affected librarianship, but rather by the constants in the profession. Characteristically, librarians are able to identify, evaluate, and make information accessible. Our ability to manage information for a diverse audience has not changed with the changes in technology. Indeed, in a world dependent on finding relevant information in a timely fashion, our skills have made us an essential part of education.

With the increased use of technology – and especially the delivery of instruction via the World Wide Web – libraries now have opportunities to extend their services to include providing library instruction and interactive reference interviews to distance learners. These opportunities come with challenges that go beyond policy for document delivery and include learning the new technologies; forming new partnerships with administrators, other instructors, and technical or computer service staff; and learning to work in an intellectual environment that is different from that of the normal on-site library. However, such challenges should not stop librarians from teaching users the skills required to locate, evaluate, and use information appropriately.

Some of our "new" partners may believe that the Web has replaced libraries – and librarians – and our task is to show them the error of their thinking. Fortunately, librarians have the skills for working in a Web-based world: we are critical and logical thinkers who are used to organizing vast arrays of information so that it can be found by novice and expert researchers alike. Furthermore, we have been in the business of communicating and disseminating information since the time of the first collection of clay tablets.

This chapter relates a specific experience to show the factors that must be considered if libraries and librarians are to be an integral part of the learning experiences of distance learners. I wish to highlight two items first. Librarians teach not mechanical skills, but intellectual skills, that is, why, when, and how to use the browser or the keyword-search button, or how to decide which periodical index to use. We teach information literacy: that set of abilities that requires individuals to recognize when information is needed and how to locate, evaluate, and use it effectively. Second, the term *distance* should be interpreted in the broadest sense. Learners, instructors, and administrators are potential users of any library instruction that might be developed for distance learners. And although distance learners are important enough to be served in their own right, many of their needs are the same as those of any individual who uses the library or seeks information without the direct involvement of a librarian, and this group includes those who do their preliminary research from their home or office before visiting the library.

Background

I am a librarian in the Queen Elizabeth II Library of Memorial University of Newfoundland (MUN), the largest university in Atlantic Canada with 16,000 full- and part-time on-campus students and 12,000 registrants in distance courses. In 1997 we decided to offer library instruction in the form of research assistance to distance education learners. As we already had a print manual for these learners, we decided to take advantage of the enthusiasm for the Web and convert the print manual to a hypertext document.

When the manual had been on the Web for a few months, we were asked to make it available to learners in other universities in the Atlantic provinces. These were all participants in the Atlantic Notemakers Project, a federally funded endeavor designed to provide learners with access to courses given by any participating university: the beginnings of a virtual university. This meant that those enrolled in a degree program with University X could take courses from any of the other universities. And while learners were taking courses from University Y, they would have access to all the services of that university, including its library services.

Following negotiations it was agreed that, under the auspices of the Council of Atlantic University Librarians/Conseil des Directeurs(trices) de Bibliothèque des Universités de l'Atlantique (CAUL/CDBUA), we at MUN would design and maintain a Web site that would give detailed research assistance. The member libraries in CAUL/CDBUA wished any new design to retain the characteristics that had originally motivated them to adopt the MUN site, that is, our plain-language strategies that connected learners to the resources they needed when they were needed. For example, when the learners were exploring the need to identify books on a topic, they were also being directed to the online catalogues that would help them complete this aspect of the research. The site can be viewed at http://www.mun.ca/library/ref/li/caul/research.html.

The challenge

Developing a Web site to address the needs of learners at six universities held many challenges, but they were similar to those that might arise in any effort to serve learners at multiple sites, for example, branches of a company or schools in a district. Although users had to agree to a common – or generic – product (the research guide itself), the various institutions did not have to share procedures or policies, such as interlibrary loan or reserve policies. Nevertheless, it was always understood that the content of the site was paramount. With this in mind we set out to develop a Web site that would:

- provide a guide to research that could be used by learners from a variety of institutions or with varying needs
- maintain the interconnectivity of the existing site so that all learners would have access to the services at their home institution
- ensure that distance learners at each institution were aware of the research assistance
- provide a Web presence that would appeal to as wide as possible a range of learning styles.

We knew that all these objectives would have to be met by existing staff: one librarian and one library technician who would add responsibility for the site to their existing workload. If specific expertise such as Hypertext Markup Language (HTML) editing or image editing were needed, those staff would find ways to acquire the needed skills. I am not an expert in HTML or image editing, but I am a survivor, and I have the scars to prove it. I learned what I know through trial and error, continuous reading, parsing Web sites, and unashamedly quizzing my friends and any expert who would talk with me. Experts can be found in a variety of places including local high schools and postsecondary institutions.

As well, at least two subtexts affected the outcome of the project: instructors would have to be willing to incorporate an element of research into their course assignments; and people from the computing support units would have to accept that a library experience was an important aspect of distance learning. The Web page would be of no value if it were not used. As basic as this sounds, it is a reality often overlooked in the rush of enthusiasm that accompanies the beginning of new projects. To ensure that the Web page would not be just an academic exercise, it was necessary to devise a strategy for developing strong, viable partnerships with a number of diverse groups that might not have been partners in other library service initiatives.

Designing library service Web sites

The Web is a popular means of delivering courses and training because it is a powerful and versatile medium that can deliver information in various formats while organizing this information through hypertext links. Good Web design is therefore imperative to render the site readily and effectively accessible to all learners.

During the initial exercise of converting a print-based research guide to a Web version, we learned much about using the Web to its fullest. The most important lesson was the three-dimensional nature of the Web. Most librarians know how to prepare two-dimensional instructional materials; they may even know how to prepare video or slide presentations and have some experience with computer-mediated learning or two-way interactive video. But these skills are not enough for the three-dimensional thinking needed for Web design, nor do the same principles for designing print-based instruction apply to designing Web-based guidance. Merely transcribing a paper document to the Web without any enhancements is of little value. The value is in adding hyperlinks to resources or help aids to further assist the user.

We realized too that connectivity is important. Access levels vary; for example, although 50 percent of Canadian households have at least one person with regular access to the Internet (Tuck 1999), access is not always equal, and not all these people have access to the Web. Variations may exist in the hardware and software used to provide this access, the amount of time access is available, and the expertise of the users. The hardware and software concerns include speed and cost of connectivity, whether learners use extensions such as a voice synthesizer, and whether they use a graphic browser (e.g., Netscape or Internet Explorer) or a nongraphical browser (e.g., lynx). The modem speed and whether users have to pay long-distance costs to connect are also relevant, as they may restrict the time learners can spend using the site. Although it is important to design the site with all users in mind – high tech and low tech – designing for the lowest common denominator does not mean sacrificing quality. Use of the Web is meant to increase accessibility to learning, not to create greater gaps between the haves and the have-nots.

Our experience reinforced the need to follow a few universal design principles (Burgstahler *et al.* 1997):

- Maintain a simple, consistent page layout throughout the site. This will make it easier for visitors to navigate through the hypertext.
- Keep backgrounds simple, and make sure there is enough contrast. This will make the text more appealing and easier to read.
- Use standard HTML, which is designed as a universal format and thus readable by all browsers.
- Include short, descriptive, alternative-textured attributes for all graphical features on the page so that those using text-only browsers can follow the links.
- Include menu alternatives for image maps (also called ISMAPS) to ensure that the embedded links are accessible to all.
- Include descriptive captions for pictures. Temporarily remove any image not considered critical, then monitor the result. If there is no impact, leave the image out.
- Caption video and transcribe other audio so that the information is accessible for those who do not have the appropriate plug-ins.
- Make links descriptive so that they are understood out of context.
- Use tables sparingly and consider alternatives to ensure that the text is available to those using text-only browsers.
- Test and consider alternatives for forms and databases; provide e-mail and other contact information for those who cannot use the forms or access the database.
- Beware of applets and plug-ins: use those that provide accessibility features that allow them to be used by text-only browsers or by users who do not have the plug-ins.

To test a site for accessibility, use Bobby (http://www.cast.org/bobby/), a Web-based tool that analyzes Web pages for their accessibility to people with disabilities. In this context, read *disabilities* to include *all* who might represent access issues.

Matters related to content and developing Web sites for the various learning styles of users must also be considered. Although this is not the place to explore the theoretical aspects of learning and pedagogy, I reflect on some of the differences between offering library instruction and reference assistance on-site as opposed to at a distance. Both services when offered in-house rely on engaging in on-the-spot, interactive communication. How librarians deliver on-the-spot services reflects their knowledge about dealing with learners in a one-on-one mode or in a classroom, so this expertise needs to be refined and translated into action that is relevant to distance learners.

Content

In library instruction classes, librarians and learners can question each other, propose alternative approaches to conducting literature searches, and offer examples based on these questions and alternatives. A central concept of a reference interview is the emphasis on the interview process – the give-and-take between user and librarian – where the underlying assumption is that not only will the person being interviewed find the information necessary to answer his or her original query, but that elements of the process itself will also be learned, thus enabling the person to develop his or her skills as an independent learner.

It is unlikely that these on-site experiences can ever be fully emulated in distance learning situations. Body language, the inflections in one's voice, the process of talking someone through the process of constructing a search: these are not easy to reproduce electronically. However, much work is being done to provide learners with the main elements of on-the-spot interactions. Sloan (1997) identifies a number of types of remote reference services and gives examples of institutions that offer these services. These efforts centered mainly on two electronic media: e-mail and/or video. He suggests a scenario where the college or university provides video reference services on a limited, scheduled basis and e-mail reference on a campus-wide, on-demand basis and elaborates on some of the problems involved in providing a remote reference service. I discuss three of them below.

Problems of remote reference services

The first problem is the potential disparity between who does the work and who benefits. The service should be set up so as to engage the learner in the reference research process. This might be done using forms that require learners to define their information needs clearly. Although the service should be created from the user's perspective, it should also incorporate the learning objectives of the reference librarians. The learner should be engaged in the critical thinking as well as the mechanical manipulation aspects of research; at the very least let them think for themselves. The second problem is the need to create a critical mass of users. It is of no use to provide a service that people cannot or will not use. For example, if the quality of the video in a reference service is poor, it will not be used. The same is true of a Web site. If an e-mail model is used, learners must have easy access to e-mail and be willing and knowledgeable enough to use it. The third problem is assignment of librarians to help learners with reference questions: the librarians must be exceptionally good at communication because there will be a number of e-mail exchanges as the learner's query is defined and refined.

These same problems should also be addressed when designing a Web site that offers research assistance. The site should guide users while giving them access to help by providing contact information. Each learner has her or his particular learning styles and needs, so a Web site needs to appeal to various approaches. Consider using site maps and links.

Develop a site map that differs from the traditional table-of-contents approach; for example, if a site offers a step-by-step cumulative approach to

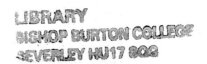

research (1. Define your topic; 2. Get background information), the site map could be designed to help users satisfy their end need (e.g., how to find books or how to find writing assistance).

Provide enough strategically located links to the site, for example, from the introductory pages of all courses and from any sites that help learners get the most out of distance education. Make sure there are links from the Web pages that learners are certain to use. Links to one's own Web pages are important, but links are also needed to external sites. In fact, this is one of the most important aspects of Web technology. Keep the links up to date and make sure they go to sites that remain relevant. Maintaining Web pages can be more time-consuming than maintaining print materials. Indeed, some people think Web pages could be the "black holes" of the modern library: spaces that absorb vast amounts of time and resources. Be sure to provide the time and personnel to keep the site current.

Even with the most user-friendly, content-rich Web site in the world the effort will have been wasted if the site is not visited and used. To ensure meaningful usage of library support services, be sure that:

- the services offered are needed and wanted (talk with partners and especially learners)
- those who should use the services, or promote their use, know that they exist (it takes time and energy to raise the awareness level of potential users; take the time, expend the energy)
- there are multiple means of accessing the information about the services ("visit" your institution as a guest).

Partnerships

It is possible to be so close and so committed to providing service that one ignores the need to secure the support of others. Significant partnerships need to be forged in order to achieve the above goals. No partnership is more important than any other, and all must operate as an integrated set during the project. Key partners for library staff are instructors, administration, and computing specialists. External groups and individuals who might be useful partners include publishers, vendors, and libraries from other sectors, for example, public and college libraries.

Distance learners are busy people and, like most of us, do not look for extra work. Many will not seek information for its own value, but for the value it will add to their immediate learning needs. In other words, unless an assignment requires evidence that learners have searched a database, acquired reading material other than what was prescribed, or somehow gone beyond the text and their own knowledge, most learners will not explore on their own. They need a reason to explore, and that reason is provided by the instructor. Librarians, therefore, must from the outset be members of any course planning and design teams, including those that develop course objectives and plan evaluation. Librarians must be proactive and win their place on these design teams.

For our Web site task, I dealt not only with people at MUN, but also with others at universities in Atlantic Canada. While these far-flung colleagues were working together as members of a virtual university, they each also had obligations to real universities. We learned that the demands of the virtual are treated as secondary when confronted by the demands of the real, and the consequent delays must be built into project schedules.

The person responsible for developing the library services must function as a spokesperson, promoter, and defender of the services, as well as carry the daily administrative duties. Awareness of the library's potential is not self-evident to non-librarians. I therefore took the time to present arguments for a greater library presence in distance learning to all the relevant and potential partners. One audience consisted of MUN colleagues from the School of Continuing Education, the university librarian, course designers, computer support staff, reference librarians, and the staff of the distance education help desk. Participants agreed that they learned more about the library than they had thought there was to learn. More important, they went on to give the library a high profile on distance education Web pages.

Effective library instruction requires a commitment of time and resources. To ensure that this commitment is at a level commensurate with needs, the services need the support of the institution's administration. With institutional budgets being tightened and many institutions experiencing downsizing, library support to distance learners must be promoted as a value-added academic service worth supporting. Although the presentation described above is a good first step, it must be followed by business plans and evidence solid enough to earn tangible support from budget administrators. The business plans should provide details of the proposed program, acknowledgment of the impact of rapidly changing technologies on staff productivity, evidence of increasing demands for continual training and learning for learners and other information researchers, and a mechanism for evaluating the effectiveness and benefits of the proposed services. Experience has taught me that it is wise to include information and statistics not only about the immediate target group – distance learners – but also about potential user groups. Any individual who uses the library or seeks information without the mediation of a librarian is a potential user of services that have been developed for distance learners. Distance is a relative term, and including these non-distance, yet still remote, users in the business plan may increase the possibility of its acceptance.

Has our collaborative Web project been a complete success? Do all instructors, administrators, and learners fully appreciate the value of information and the library? I wish this were the case. However, my goal is not to achieve perfection, but to use contemporary technologies to further traditional library service values of equity of access, personal service, and service tailored to individual needs. At the end of the day I do not want to hear myself reciting the words from the morning prayer in the Anglican *Book of Common Prayer*: "We have left undone those things which we ought to have done, and we have done those things which we ought not to have done."

Guidelines for effective practice

1   *Focus on user needs.* Much can be done that is neither needed nor wanted. Know what is needed and provide it.
2   *Assess time and commitment.* Never underestimate how long it will take to learn how to use new technology effectively. But when you do, persevere, as you will have already invested too much time and energy to quit.
3   *Partner, partner, partner.* Form partnerships with obvious and traditional partners, but do not ignore the non-traditional and the hitherto unrelated. Use imagination to think of new partners.
4   *Make content dictate form.* Be sure that content dictates form, not the other way around. The medium may be important, but the message is still why you are communicating.
5   *Keep it simple.* There is a fine line between making technology work for learners and creating a gap between those who can and those who cannot become learners. Be sure to use a version of technology that is usable by all target learners.
6   *Maximize the technology.* If the technology offers something new, take advantage of it, for example, use hyperlinks in Web-based documents.
7   *Get the word out.* Let others know what you have done and how it will benefit them. As with partnerships, consider communicating with groups and individuals that might not have traditionally been considered.

References

American Library Association (1998) *ACRL Guidelines for Distance Learning Library Services* (Approved July 1998). Online. Available: http://www.ala.org/acrl/guides/distlrng.html.
Burgstahler, S., Comden, D., and Fraser, B. (1997) "Universal Access: Designing and Evaluating Web Sites for Accessibility," *Choice*, Supplement, 19–22.
Canadian Library Association (n.d.) *Guidelines for Library Support of Distance and Distributed Learning in Canada* (draft). Online. Available: http://gateway1.uvic.ca/dls/guidelines.html.
Sloan, B. (1997) *Service Perspectives for the Digital Library: Remote Reference Services*. Online. Available: http://www.lis.uiuc.edu/~b-sloan/e-ref.html (December 16).
Tuck, S. (1999) "Internet Milestone Set as 50% Connected in Canada," *Globe and Mail*, May 1, B1, B11.

Bibliography

Austen, G. (1998) "Libraries in Partnership: Defining Our Core Roles for the 21st Century," in *The Challenge to be Relevant in the 21st Century: Proceedings of the International Association of Technological University Libraries (IATUL) Conference.* Online. Available: http://educate.lib.chalmers.se/IATUL/proceedcontents/pretpap/austen.html.

Balas, J.L. (2000) "Doing it Right: Web Design for Library Types," *Computers in Libraries*, 20, 1, 56–59.

Burge, E.J. and Snow, J.E. (2000) "Candles, Corks and Contracts: Essential Relationships Between Learners and Librarians," *New Review of Libraries and Lifelong Learning*, 1, 1, 19–34.

Chute, A.G., Thompson, M.M., and Hancock, B.W. (1999) *The McGraw-Hill Handbook of Distance Learning.* New York: McGraw-Hill.

Dewald, N., Scholz-Crane, A., Booth, A., and Levine, C. (2000) "Information Literacy at a Distance: Instructional Design Issues," *Journal of Academic Librarianship*, 26, 1, 33–44.

Gray, S.M. (2000) "Virtual Reference Services: Directions and Agendas," *Reference and User Services Quarterly*, 39, 4, 365–375.

Jones, D. (1998) Critical Thinking in an Online World. *Proceedings of the Untangling the Web Conference.* Online. Available: http://www.library.ucsb.edu/untangle/jones.html.

Jones, M. (1997) "High Five for the Next Five: Librarians and Distance Education," *Journal of Library Services for Distance Education*, 1, 1. Online. Available: http://www.westga.edu/~library/jlsde/jlsde

Libutti, P.O. (1999) *Librarians as Learners, Librarians as Teachers: The Diffusion of Internet Expertise in the Academic Library.* Chicago: American Library Association.

McGlamery, S. and Coffman, S. (2000) "Moving Reference to the Web," *Reference and User Services Quarterly*, 39, 4, 380–386.

Slade, A.L. and Kascus, M. (2000) *Library Services for Open and Distance Learning: The Third Bibliography.* Englewood, CO: Libraries Unlimited.

Starkweather, W.M. and Wallin, C.C. (1999) "Faculty Response to Library Technology: Insights on Attitudes," *Library Trends*, 47, 4, 640–668.

Straw, J.E. (2000) "A Virtual Understanding: The Reference Interview and Question Negotiation in the Digital Age," *Reference and User Services Quarterly*, 39, 4, 376–379.

Terkla, D. and McKinzie, S. (1997) "The Revolution is Being Televised: Pedagogy and Information Retrieval in the Liberal Arts College," *College and Undergraduate Libraries*, 4, 2, 9–20.

Wallach, R. (1997) "An Embarrassment of Riches," in A.L. Duda (ed.) *The Universe at Your Fingertips: Continuing Web Education.* (ERIC document ED 412898.) Online. Available: http://www.library.ucsb.edu/universe/wallach.html.

World Wide Web Consortium (W3C) (2001) *Web Content Accessibility Guidelines 2.0. CW3C Recommendation.* Online. Available: http://www.w3.org/TR/WCAG201

9 "No one will listen to us": Rural Fulbe women learning by radio in Nigeria

Lantana Usman

As a professor at Ahmadu Bello University in Nigeria and head of a social studies teacher education unit that includes distance education for rural students, I have long been concerned with issues of women's learning through various technologies. My involvement with the nomadic women began when I was a research assistant conducting research on issues of health care, sanitation, maternal delivery, and food and nutrition. In this work, I was struck by how the women responded to my questions by referring to educational radio programs they had heard. So for this chapter, my focus is women's involvement with the radio programs and the constraints they face in listening to them. Radio can be a useful learning medium for people in many different urban and rural contexts and regions (Tahir 1991; Mitchell and Murugan 2000; Walker and Dhanarajan 2000; Maskow 2001), but its effectiveness depends on context- and learner-sensitive planning and delivery.

To augment my family income, I often drive from the city to the rural markets to buy grains. On one of my visits, I parked near a section where the nomadic women were concentrated; it is referred to in Hausa as *kasuwan mataal sashin ya'n nono*, the market section for women. The women were selling dairy products and at the same time chatting and commenting on a radio program being broadcast in Fulfulde, the language of the Fulbe nomads. The women had positioned their radios on the lids of their calabashes (the large gourds used as containers). Their comments made me curious. I moved closer, introduced myself in Fulfulde, and asked them a general question concerning their views on the radio program. The women, who identified themselves as Hanne, Saáde, and Laminde, responded positively. First, they affirmed their appreciation of the program in their own language and were proud that their language and tribal identity were recognized and heard locally and worldwide. As one of them remarked, "No one knows the Fulani. Only when they [other ethnic groups] want to buy our cattle for food, then they realize we exist, but now the government has made our people known throughout Nigeria and around the world." In addition, they appreciated the concerns of the federal government for them as an ethnic group.

"Are you satisfied with the contents of the programs broadcast in Fulfulde?" I asked. They liked all the programs, they told me, and wished that they could see as well as hear some of the dramas. As Hanne added about the main comic character in one of the radio drama programs they enjoyed, "I want to see the woman called Filani in the *Samanja* series; I guess she will be even funnier!" I then asked how much it cost to purchase the radios. They laughed and sighed. Hanne commented, "I didn't buy the radio; I got it from my husband who got a new radio which he purchased at a subsidized rate with the assistance of the [men's cattle breeders] association." "And why weren't the women included in this allocation?" Laminde responded, "No one will listen to us in any case if our husbands are taken care of, *Alhamdudillahi* [Thanks be to God]."

I pondered the incident. I wondered at the educational efficacy of the women's listening when they were also selling their produce. I enjoyed their comments on the content they heard and the animated discussions they held among themselves. But Laminde's comment stayed with me: "No one will listen to us."

The nomadic Fulbe women

The Fulbe are an indigenous, predominantly pastoral people who herd cattle in northern Nigeria. They constitute about 3 million people, about 2.6 percent of Nigeria's total population (Tahir 1998). The Fulbe are composed of clans, each of which occupies specific zones for pastoral herding. The women participate in all aspects of animal husbandry and travel with their families during the seasonal migrations.

The status of nomadic Fulbe women is similar to that of other African rural women: "household managers, providing food, nutrition, water, health, education and family planning" (Odedra-Straub 1995: 261). Significantly, they are predominantly Muslim, so their life is bound by Islamic doctrines and practices. However, the concept of purdah – total seclusion of women often symbolized by the veil – is seldom practiced by these women because they are involved in various economic activities. Besides running their households, they are entrepreneurs in the processing and marketing of perishable milk, butter, yogurt, and allied products (De St Croix 1972). They control milk production, manipulate its sale, and make money as traders. Financial interest accrued from trading belongs to the women; their spouses have no right to it even though they own the cattle. However, the women spend most of the profits on their families' daily needs. Gustafsson noted that "they save money and buy necessary items such as salt, kerosene for the lamps in the home, cooking oils and spices" (1991: 14). They also buy clothes for themselves and their children. Their economic strength has given them social empowerment, as well as respect from their husbands and other family members. However, in educational matters, which are still often viewed as imbued with Western values, the husband still controls access and participation even to formal radio-based education. The women are dependent on the men for access to the radio and permission to purchase one.

These women are visible traders in their localities. Their interest in market trading is based not only on economic purposes, but also as a means to socialize with other people. As Gustafsson reported: "for tribals going to weekly market is like ritual. They wear their best clothes and walk up to ten kilometers or more to the market, as most families have something for sale" (1991: 14). Trips to the market enable them to meet with other women, participate in market gossip about each other, and discuss social issues like marriages, weddings, divorces, deaths, and births (De St Croix 1972). Furthermore, it enables the women to obtain the latest information about new markets with greater demands for milk and other dairy products. This enables them to plan marketing strategies and to increase the capacity of production to meet the demand of consumers in such target markets.

Of all the Muslim women in northern Nigeria, the Fulbe nomadic women enjoy the greatest trading independence in the form of outdoor sales and management of financial profits. However, access to modern financial capital is difficult for them. Because of their low literacy level and lack of information about available credit facilities such as rural banking, most nomadic women have not used such facilities. Instead, they continue to practice the traditional credit system *adashe*, which is based on group members' contributions. It is a means of generating financial capital by providing women in a rural economy with access to private or public credit from outside sources (Bullock 1994).

Most Fulbe women have encountered information technology through their transistor radios and cassette recorders. Typically, these are first introduced into the family by the head of household. The fact that women possessed radios became the official rationale for prescribing and implementing use of the radio as an instructional strategy in the distance education or outreach program for them (Federal Republic of Nigeria 1989). Fulbe women have informal contact with television and films through government documentary and other programs developed by institutions such as the universities. In most documentaries on rural women in developing countries, the women are presented as political news items that portray them as beneficiaries of various welfare programs or projects (Krishnan and Dighe 1990; Patel 1997).

The level of literacy among the Fulbe nomadic women is low; most cannot read or write in Fulbe or Hausa. Instead, their literacy is based on their indigenous knowledge. When Western education was introduced to the nomads in the early 1970s, they initially resented it and saw it as sabotaging their mode of production in subsistence animal husbandry. They fled in an attempt to escape from authorities who were bent on enforcing the then new Universal Primary Education (UPE) regulations. They feared that the settled majority would use universal education as a means to enforce settlement and conformity on them (Junaid 1987).

Subsequently, the attitude of the nomadic Fulbe in Nigeria to Western education has changed, and this is seen in their efforts to acquire modern education. The earliest adult education centers, which were opened in Bauchi in 1972, were established by the local men's cattle breeders' association. Ten years later in 1982, nomadic men in the Bassa local government started a similar program for women at Huke, a village near Miango. At that time the curriculum of the self-assisted program for women centered on basic reading and writing skills taught on-site in a classroom. This program reached only a small number of women.

The National Commission for Nomadic Education

The National Commission for Nomadic Education was established in December 1989 to implement the government's *Nomadic Education Policy Blueprint* (Federal Republic of Nigeria 1987). Part of the policy focuses on adult literacy programs for Fulbe nomadic women. Literacy and numeracy program outcomes are based on the acquisition of skills relevant to the production and marketing of dairy products, as well as on their maternal responsibilities. The rationale behind the programs is to provide functional knowledge and skills so as to empower them to improve themselves and contribute meaningfully to the development of their communities.

The *Nomadic Education Blueprint* (Federal Republic of Nigeria 1987) noted that because nomadic lives combine periods of sedentary life with migration in search of pasture for their herds, no single system was adequate to provide them with meaningful education. The Commission recommended various approaches for educating women in the outreach literacy programs, but most of the emphasis has been on their continuing to use the radio and their meetings in the markets (Ezeomah 1998). Most nomadic Fulbe families consider the radio a necessity. It is not uncommon to see pastoral women traveling to market centers with small portable radios on the covers of their calabashes, as described in the opening story.

Ezeomah (1983), an authority on Fulbe educational studies, traced the history of nomadic Fulbe educational programming to Plateau, one of the states in Nigeria, the government of which in 1981 established the Nomadic Fulani Educational Broadcasts in order to encourage the nomads toward social change. Most radio education programs emphasize certain aspects of nomadic work roles such as prevention of certain animal diseases. To educate the nomads, the broadcasts were designed not only to be heard, but also to stimulate reflection and reaction in the Fulbe. Thus their general awareness of events around them would be awakened, and they would be able to participate fully in their education because the broadcasts would bring knowledge of areas that affected their daily life.

Despite the popularity of the radio education broadcasts in Plateau state, and even though women made up 31 percent of listeners (Ezeomah 1983), the content of the broadcasts focused mainly on issues for Fulbe men. Because the current policy of nomadic education has recently become a national concern, the Commission has emphasized the need for more programming for

Fulbe women. This would empower them, as well as assist them to increase the productivity of their cheese, milk, and butter businesses. They have also begun to offer workshops for the women on radio: listening skills and implementation of the radio information in their lives ("Survey of Radio Kaduna" 1998).

The curriculum of radio-based education

The Nomadic Education Policy (NEP) curriculum, which is the basis of the radio programs, comprises topics such as child and maternal health care, modern means of milk processing and hygiene, water purification and sanitation, food and nutrition (emphasizing the use of local, affordable ingredients), and basic skills in handicrafts (Hajiya 1997). In addition, reading and writing skills are taught through some community development programs.

The curriculum of the radio programs can be divided into four main areas: educational topics, general information programs, religious education, and entertainment. The educational programs are usually didactic in format and include programs like *Njamu Ma* (Health Talks), which inform listeners about the nature, symptoms, prevention, and treatment of some common diseases, *Ngam Wainabe e Remobe* (For Farmers and Cattle Rearers), which provides useful information about animal and crop practices, and *Filin Girken Mu*, a cooking and nutrition program (Umar 1987).

The general information broadcasts use a wider variety of formats from quiz programs to magazine-style interviews and commentary. Examples include a quiz program *Babal Kisol* (Brains Trust), current affairs programs such as *Ko Ngida* (Who Do You See?), and *Kita Dareju Mon* (Answers to Listeners' Questions). The magazine-type programs have no set content, but are based on the interests of the producer and topical issues.

Religious programs provide either Muslim sermons or educational programs such as *Yamde e jawabuji Dina Lislama* (Questions and Answers on Islam).

The entertainment programs most often highlight cultural and social issues of socialization, morality, and civic responsibilities. They range from *Yakeji Amin* (In Our Days), which talks about social change by comparing contemporary life with "life in the old days" to drama series like *Samanja*.

Program design

The educational programs are designed to be self-instructional. For those involving reading and writing, the materials are sent to the students, the radio speaker provides do-it-yourself instructions, and evaluation methods are implemented at the end of the series. When the students run into difficulties, they are supposed to write to the radio station, and the response will be broadcast on the Answers to Listeners' Questions program.

The women usually gather together to listen to the programs. This group form of interaction, discussion, and knowledge-sharing is common among the Fulbe. Umar (1987) found that educational and religious programs were less popular than the other types. Possible reasons for this are that such programs are too didactic. The mode of presentation is normally an expert lecturing to the audience or an expert being interviewed. Such programs tend to impart too much information in too short a time. Umar commented that such programs are too intellectual and do not relate well to the listeners' everyday lives. Other constraints and problems include the often lengthy delays in the arrival of materials, the lack of any personal feedback as radio answers usually combine many questions in one response, and the contention that the radio announcers ignore questions related to women's programs.

Timing

Four radio stations broadcast regular programs in Fufulde for two to seven hours per week. Most programs are repeated on another day. Programs broadcast early in the morning or late in the evening have a large audience. However, the educational programs are often broadcast at noon or mid-afternoon when many women are traveling to or from market or are busy with customers, as I have observed in my visits to the local markets.

Despite these problems, many women appreciate the educational radio programs. An independent survey on the impact and relevance of the educational series from Radio Kaduna revealed that both the women and the men agreed that the entire program has had a positive effect on their lives (Hajiya 1997). As one of the women in my story commented, "Now the government has made our people [Fulbe] known throughout Nigeria and around the world [through the radio]." The women interviewed in the survey expressed the need for more information on animal and child care, improved ways of milking, preservation of milk and commercialization, health care, and the teaching of more vocational skills (Hajiya 1997).

Radio education for nomads has become essential given their low level of literacy (0.02 percent, of which women constitute the majority, Ezeomah 1998). It has numerous advantages over the mobile schools that have been set up near certain grazing encampments. In particular, it should enable the Commission to overcome the problems of shortage of teachers and poor retention of learners, because neither teachers nor students of these schools stay for long (Tahir 1998). As observed in some grazing camps, the radio education hour, especially in the evenings when all are resting from their work, brings the entire family together as they listen and later evaluate their level of comprehension through questions and answers among the group members. Hence radio education broadcasts can enable self-evaluation, increase inquiry, and be critically thought-provoking for the nomad listeners.

Listening to the women

I am spurred to ask: What can I learn from the women in the market and their involvement in the radio programs? My first reaction is that the nomadic women use the radio frequently and are engaged by the programs because they talk among themselves, as well as develop and remember what they have listened to in postprogram discussions. I believe the radio is the most convenient technology for their distance learning, but to my mind much more needs to be done if radio is to realize its potential for teaching the nomadic women. Several significant issues need to be addressed, and, as I mull them over, I realize that these have implications for my own distance education work.

The first major issue is immediately evident in the market story: these women have to make time for education in addition to their regular work. As well, the radio broadcast times do not take into consideration the rhythm of the women's lives. The issue of timing often appears in my own work when the university schedule conflicts with the ongoing demands of female learners. It reminds me that we need to pay less attention to our own requirements and try to provide more flexibility for learners' choices.

The second major issue is learner-relevant learning activities. The radio education programs do not reflect or enhance the learning strategies of the nomadic women. Like many women in distance education (Burge 1998; von Prümmer 2000), they prefer to learn together, and so often spend time discussing what they have heard. Producers of educational programs need to reconceptualize educational programs and reconsider what sources of information their listeners pay attention to and retain: for example, having more women as participant discussants as well as teachers on the radio programs. Including women in this way would motivate other female learners, as well as help maintain the focus on topics relevant to their daily concerns. The rather rigid pedagogy of the radio programs is described as too intellectual (Umar 1987) and needs to be changed to a more socially interactive approach, which would be especially welcome in subjects like religious education, simple arithmetic, and bookkeeping, which are often taught by the same radio teacher. Understandably, the women become bored as they listen to the same voice for all lessons. The didactic style too could be reconceptualized to situate learning tasks within the realities of the learners' daily lives: for example, using drama to teach subjects related to the women's market trading activities (arithmetic), child care, and maternal health care. Such a pedagogical planning approach would enable greater success and better timing of the curriculum, as well as elicit more interest from the women in these subjects. Here is another example.

In my contact with the nomadic women in the markets, I often observed a language barrier in their dealings with customers. Those who cannot speak Fulfulde or Hausa, which the women also understand and use, find it difficult to transact business with them. Sometimes such a language barrier can lead customers to take unfair advantage of them, especially in the use of measurement units for selling their products. Teaching them market entrepreneur education in measurements and basic English would enable the women to explore wider markets and also help them to avoid being cheated in their business activities.

How, then, can educators help to maintain the women's interest in learning as well as their ongoing use of radio technology? Many answers must lie with the National Commission for Nomadic Education. In order to achieve its aims for the Interactive Radio Education Program (IREP) begun in 1998, the Commission and local radio producers need to include more educational programs that actively involve women and relate more closely to their earning activities and their unpaid work. The resulting programs should include education on promoting the quality and quantity of the women's primary economic resource, dairy management, which in fact is stated as one of the objectives of the IREP (Tahir and Umar 1999).

From this outline of the key issues, it is clear to me that the Commission needs to consult adequately with the nomadic women themselves. The women should be involved in the planning and production of radio learning programs, as was noted quite some years ago by Ezeomah (1983) in a survey that revealed that 93 percent of nomad respondents (men and women) wished to communicate with program producers. But the very mobility of the nomads means that such communication must be facilitated through field workers. Once contact is made, the field staff could help ensure that any radio program is designed to reflect the cultural background and priorities of the nomads. Additional ways to improve the educational impact of the programs are to tell the women about the programs and to broadcast them at times that do not conflict with household work.

It also seems that the Commission's management consults with the women's cooperative groups or social organizations less often than it does with the men's associations. Much attention has been given to the men's Cattle Breeders' Association, and the Commission does consult them on educational matters. They have received more support not only in the number of male-oriented programs, but also in the purchase of radios at subsidized rates. This marginalizes the women, although the women's groups do not have a common united front that parallels the men's association. This marginalization has made the women take a defeatist position as illustrated by Laminde in my opening story, "No one will listen to us." Although such a position is understandable, it may demotivate women from participating in educational radio programs.

Access to any form of education favors the role of men as heads of households, and it is they who control access and participation of women by retaining the power of consent. In addition, as noted in the opening story, the women depend on the men to purchase or introduce the radio into the family. Development experts working in the developing world have sometimes assumed that if technology is extended to the head of the family, others in the household will benefit. This may be a false assumption because in many households women are often the last to be consulted or actively involved. Unhelpful approaches by these developmental experts and the Commission staff that are insensitive to women's concerns, therefore, actively repress women and act as a means to reinforce the existing patriarchal norms that marginalize rural women.

Guidelines for assessing programs

1   Does the program fit the life demands of the learners? Does it take account of the life demands of women learners?
2   Have the learners been consulted about the design and ongoing implementation of the program? Have women learners been consulted and given choices about program aspects?
3   Is there a regular opportunity for learners to be involved in the overall program policies? Is there a regular opportunity for women to be involved?
4   Has the position of women been considered? Is the pedagogy appropriate? Does it reflect cultural norms?
5   How are women presented in the programs? Are there role models to encourage women's participation?

In conclusion, I wish to point out that despite all the issues and conditions outlined above, the radio education programs have great potential to stimulate the women's learning and "conscientize" them as a group to how various societal inequities operate and create awareness (Freire 1970). This calls for educators and administrators who will listen more closely to the women, who will take them seriously, and who will recognize how they struggle with energy and conviction to counteract the inequities and to construct learning conditions appropriate to their needs.

References

Bullock, S. (1994) *Women and Work*. London: Zed Books.
Burge, E.J. (1998) "Gender in Distance Education," in C.C. Gibson (ed.) *Distance Learners in Higher Education*. Madison, WI: Atwood.
De St Croix, F.W. (1972) *The Fulani of Northern Nigeria*. Farnborough: Gregg International.
Ezeomah, C. (1983) *The Education of Nomadic People: The Fulani of Northern Nigeria*. Hull: Oriel Press.
Ezeomah, C. (1998) "Distance Education for Nomads," in G. Tahir and N.D. Muhammad (eds) *Readings in Distance Education for the Pastoral Nomads of Nigeria*. Zaria: Ahmadu Bello University Press.
Federal Republic of Nigeria (1987) *Nomadic Education Policy Blueprint*. Lagos: Federal Government of Nigeria Printer.
Federal Republic of Nigeria (1989) *National Commission for Nomadic Education. Decree 41 of 12 December*. Lagos: Federal Government of Nigeria Printer.

Freire, P. (1970) *Pedagogy of the Oppressed*. New York: Seabury Press.

Gustafsson, U. (1991) *Can Literacy Lead to Development?* Arlington, TX: Summer Institute of Linguistics and the University of Texas.

Hajiya, J.H. Ali (1997) "Women Form Nomadic Women Co-operatives and North-East Zone 46 Nomadic Women in Ningi Embrace Education," *Nomadic Education News*, 4, 1, 12.

Junaid, M. (1987) "Education and Cultural Integrity: An Ethnographic Study of the Problems of Formal Education and Pastoralist Families in Sokoto State, Nigeria." Unpublished doctoral dissertation, York University.

Krishnan, P. and Dighe, A. (1990) *Affirmation and Denial: Construction of Femininity on Indian Television*. New Delhi: Sage.

Maskow, M. (2001) "Radio as a Learning Technology," in E.J. Burge (ed.) *The Strategies of Use of Learning Technologies, New Directions for Adult and Continuing Education No. 88*. San Francisco, CA: Jossey-Bass.

Mitchell, B. and Murugan, K. (2000) *The Use of Public Broadcasting in the Caribbean for Open/Distance Learning*, Unpublished report for The Commonwealth of Learning. http://www.col.org/Consultancies/00caribfeas.htm.

National Commission for Nomadic Education (2000) *Action Plan, 1996–2000*. Lagos: Federal Government of Nigeria Printer.

Odedra-Straub, M. (ed.) (1995) *Global Information Technology and Socio-economic Development*. Nashua: Ivy League.

Patel, I. (1997) "Women in Popular Culture: Television and Film," in L.J. Peach (ed.) *Women in Popular Culture*. Oxford: Blackwell.

"Survey of Radio Kaduna" (1998) *Nomadic Education News*, 5, 1, 16.

Tahir, G. (1991) "Radio for Development Communication Among the Fulbe in Nigeria," in G. Tahir (ed.) *Education and Pastoralism in Nigeria*. Zaria: Ahmadu Bello University Press.

Tahir, G. (1998) "Nomadic Education in Nigeria: Issues, Problems, and Prospects," *Journal of Nomadic Studies*, 1, 1, 10–26.

Tahir, G. and Umar, A. (1999) "Distance Learning for the Provision of Access to the Unreached and the Minorities: The Case of the Distance Learning Scheme for Nomadic Pastoralists in Nigeria." Paper presented at the regional seminar on the development of collaborative projects in distance education, Nigeria National Commission for UNESCO, University of Ibadan.

Umar, A. (1987) "The Planning of Radio for Adult Education among the Pastoralist Fulani: A Reconstructionist Approach." Unpublished doctoral dissertation, University College of Wales, Aberystwyth.

von Prümmer, C. (2000) *Women in Distance Education*. London: Routledge.

Walker, D. and Dhanarajan, G. (2000) "Community Radio." Unpublished manuscript. Online. Available: http://www.col.org/speeches/00EFA.htm.

10 Confronting barriers to distance study in Tanzania

Edith Mhehe

Although the general mission of the Open University of Tanzania (OUT, established in 1994) is to enhance adults' access to education, in 1996 President Benjamin Mkapa announced that the OUT's special mission is to promote the education of Tanzanian women, because their only hope of attaining higher education is by the distance mode (Mkapa 1996). Despite efforts to attract female students, the extent of women's participation in tertiary education in Tanzania is limited: for the OUT only 12 percent, 683 women of the total population of 5,689 students (Ministry of Science, Technology and Higher Education 1999). As a faculty member and Dean of Education (1994–96) of the OUT since its establishment, and since, I have been concerned at the low participation rates for women. I believe that unless the OUT fully understands the underlying causes of women's low enrollment, inadequate participation, and unacceptable completion rates, it will be unable to adjust its planning, managerial, and administrative procedures to provide appropriate learning opportunities for women.

During 1999 and 2000, when I traveled to various regional and local OUT study centers, I met with over 80 women students and nonstudents and listened to and tape-recorded their stories. What I heard has helped me understand the extent of the challenge for the OUT in its goal to enhance and sustain women's access and academic success. I describe the OUT system below in order to put the challenges in these stories in context.

Background

The Open University of Tanzania serves an area of 945,000 km². Its teaching and learning system is based on print learning materials and two written assignments, but also includes an orientation and two face-to-face tutoring sessions, science laboratory sessions or teaching practical, two timed tests, and an annual and supplementary examination (if required) in each course (OUT 2000). These activities occur in the 25 regional centers, which also provide limited library services; to reach them, often across long distances, students need enough money to pay for transportation, accommodation, food, and any medical care. There are also 56 local centers, some in each region, where students meet subject peer groups and their tutors. The print course materials are delivered to students mainly by postal services, but also through public carriers and via the OUT staff during their visits to the regional centers. Plans are underway (as of October 2000) to use the regional centers as the main venues for storing and distributing study materials (Mmari 1997). The OUT buys study materials from other distance learning universities in Nairobi, Zimbabwe, South Africa, Abuja, and India and has published 84 of its own courses, written by faculty staff from Tanzanian universities and other post-secondary institutions. The OUT has four faculties and two institutes with a total of 45 staff (OUT 2000).

The women's stories

The stories I heard dealt directly with the everyday realities of the female students' lives. Many had had to overcome time constraints, cultural expectations, and financial obstacles regarding their higher education. I discuss each in turn.

Time constraints

> All the time I feel tired due to too much work. If I try to study, I feel sleepy. If I force myself to study, I find myself reading with very little understanding because the brain and the body are tired. They need some rest, but I cannot rest because at 5.30 in the morning I am required to be up again to prepare for the family breakfast and go to a full day's work.

A fourth-year student told me that since she enrolled with the OUT, she was compelled to study in the brief periods between her chores and other demands in her life. This tired her and was a contributing factor to her poor academic performance. She protested that in addition to her tight family and work schedules, she had to be away approximately 85 days per year to attend compulsory study activities at the regional center (OUT 2000). While away from her family and employment, she had to pay for transportation, food, accommodation, and health care. She also had to make trips to libraries for books and journals and to the local study center to find course colleagues and part-time tutors to discuss the difficult parts of her studies.

A fourth-year student in law complained that many students did not receive their study materials, yet the OUT demanded that they pay full fees. She commented on the OUT's "lopsided " service provision saying, "This is one-way traffic!" Many other women told similar stories about the difficulties of obtaining study materials on time and then having enough time at home to study. They saw these time problems as barriers that discouraged many women from even enrolling with the OUT, explaining that a major reason why most enrolled women abandoned their studies was their inability to meet the logistical demands placed on them by the system.

When I asked about the possible use of alternative learning technologies, one woman suggested that her most pressing need was not for learning technologies, but for other technologies such as washing machines, cookers, and vacuum cleaners, which could help shorten the time she spent on housework and increase the time she needed for studying. Her answer applies to many female students at the OUT.

These factors have serious implications for the OUT. First is the time-stressed position of the Tanzanian woman who is entirely responsible for all household tasks. In many situations, not only does she run the household, hold a full-time job, and look after the children, but she is also responsible for small farming projects such as raising chickens or cows or tilling gardens and fields to augment her income. Many women who seek OUT courses see a university degree as a means to improve their economic status. But little time for study is available for women unless family members help them.

Cultural expectations

> If the husbands would allow their wives freedom to make decisions for their own lives and act on them, many women would be studying with the OUT by combining their multiple roles in whatever circumstances are possible in their families.

Many stories convinced me of the accuracy of this statement from a young female would-be student. I first met this young schoolteacher with her daughter when I visited her regional center. On my second visit some months later, I learned that although she had registered with the OUT and paid the initial sum of 60 percent of the total fees, she had failed to start her studies because her husband refused to give her permission. When I tried to get him to change his mind he told me, "At the moment she has so many other family responsibilities, and if she starts now there will be nobody to take care of the family." He further argued that if she began studies, she would concentrate on them and have no time to think about family matters. At another center I heard from a primary schoolteacher who was married with five children. She complained that her efforts to be a student had been stifled after only six months of struggle. Her husband prevented her from doing anything on weekends other than taking care of family responsibilities: the children, the cows, the farm, receiving visitors, and visiting.

> He would say, "Ah, ah, school work! This you can do other days when I am not home. When I am home, I do not like you to do that." You see! So I cannot study at all when he is at home, and I could not attend [the regional center].

On several evenings when she wanted to study he turned off the lights claiming that the electricity bills were too high and demanded that she study in the daytime. But with teaching all day and doing family chores in the evening, she had little time or energy left to study. One regional director told me of cases where the men picked up their wives' study materials and did not allow them to participate in the learning activities. Any attempt to negotiate with a husband to allow his wife to participate in the activities generally led to termination of the wife's studies.

Traditional cultures and some religious practices in Tanzania empower men (husbands, fathers, brothers, grandfathers, or uncles) to control female relatives in all aspects of their lives. Women (wives, mothers, sisters, grand-mothers, or aunts) are not allowed to take any action or make any final decision that might affect their lives or those of others, including other women or children in their families. Through culture and socialization, most women are taught that husbands and other men will not participate in any tasks or roles usually ascribed to women. Many women thus unquestioningly carry out all the unpaid family work, their paid work in employment, and other life tasks such as studying. Without their husbands' permission they cannot use their own money to enroll with the OUT or to participate in the activities at the study centers. Tanzanian laws and society have retained a traditional division of labor to the extent that a Tanzanian woman may not sue a man for family support and child care expenses. Even with changes in the law the men, especially in rural areas, tend to follow the traditional power structure. Despite the recent land reform bill passed in the National Assembly early in 1999, research reports show that "still in the Kilimanjaro area, customary practices continue to reckon land along lines that are independent of the bill" (Stambach 2000: 178); that is, women are still barred from owning land.

The stories the women told me indicate that the OUT has not yet provided a flexible and convenient distance education system suitable for Tanzanian women who live under this culture of male domination. They complained that they faced "unique-to-women" (*shida za wanawake*) difficulties when they tried to participate in OUT studies, particularly those at the regional and local study centers. For example, the women have to travel to the centers, which are in towns usually some distance from their homes. But for cultural and religious reasons, rented accommodations (guest houses or hotels) in towns are not considered respectable places for women to stay without their spouses. Social mores claim this is for the women's own safety and protection. In fact it enables the men to exercise their authoritative power over the women by denying them permission to participate or spend funds on rented accommo-dation and by requiring them to be unquestioningly obedient to male family members.

An even more sensitive issue is that when they are in the centers the women have to interact often and over several days with their tutors (often male) and study with male students. This situation has prevented many women from enrolling with the OUT because their husbands will not allow them to participate under such conditions. Nor can the women easily ask permission of their husbands as they themselves understand the culture and abide by its traditional restrictions (Mbughuni 1994; Synder and Tadesse 1995). Additional constraints on choices for women students may arise in the workplace: female employees need to negotiate frequent absences from work, but many women have told me that their male bosses demand "personal" favors as a condition to giving permission for the absence. Complying with such demands could severely damage both their marriages and their health (i.e., HIV/AIDS).

Taking examinations and tests presents further logistical challenges to OUT women. The long distances, the uncertain state of the country's transportation system, and the pressure to take the least time possible away from family and work cause difficulty for many women. At present a student who misses the tests must wait to write supplementary examinations (sometimes up to three months). This delays a woman's ongoing studies or may extinguish her motivation to continue her education.

Financial resources

> I saw there was a chance for me to do my university studies with the OUT. I applied right away and they sent me their form explaining the procedures for enrolling. One of them is paying 70,000 Tanzanian shillings [Ts] per year for tuition fees, something I knew right away I could not afford because I am still paying for my children's education, and other needs in the family including my bus fare to work. So I quitted the idea right away.

This young woman had wanted to become an OUT student, but she could not meet the required 60 percent of the annual fee that must be paid before students receive any study materials. The total fee is Ts120,000, more than many women can afford from their salaries. The average salary of a woman with the requisite high school completion or diploma qualifications to apply to the OUT would be between Ts35,000 and Ts90,000 per month. The annual fee is much more than they can save from their small household money-making projects. For widows or single mothers with young children, the costs become prohibitive. A fourth-year student and mother lamented:

> Their father has died, and the whole burden is left to me. The pension he had is so small, and my monthly Ts50,000 salary cannot cover much when I also have to pay the house rent in town, pay for three children's private secondary school, and for food and medicines. Unless OUT can provide free education for women, women will still fail to seize the educational opportunity provided by the OUT.

As well as the initial course fee, the women must also pay for the compulsory trips to the regional and study centers. A fifth-year student from Hanang explained her costs for one trip to the closest center with subject peers and a tutor.

> To attend a one-day face-to-face session in Dodoma I must have not less than Ts100,000 if I don't have a relative to stay with. With a relative, I normally spend about Ts50,000. From Hanang town where I live to Dodoma the return ticket alone is about Ts30,000 because I normally pay Ts15,000 one way. The other Ts20,000 I spend for my needs and local transport in Dodoma town itself.

Many women described their attempts to obtain enough funds to pay for their enrollment at the OUT. Although a few were supported by a husband or male relative, many others had to save a few shillings at a time until they had enough to pay the fee. It was not clear to me whether many women were fully informed of the costs extra to the tuition fees at the time of enrollment. Many told me that their difficulties in understanding the course materials were eclipsed by their continual need for enough money to continue their studies. In many cases their savings were enough only to take one course at a time; and even then personal and family circumstances could completely derail their plans.

I was surprised at how many of the OUT women students I met were widows, single parents, Catholic sisters, unmarried women in their late 30s and early 40s, or women whose husbands had retired. In each of the regional centers I visited, more than half the students belonged to these groups. Ironically, although the tuition costs are a serious hardship for these mainly single salary earners, their life circumstances have freed them from male control.

I am glad I decided to talk to the women about their experiences with enrolling and studying at the OUT. Their stories made me admire their determination, cry at their frustration, and feel anger at the systemic discrimination inscribed in the OUT operations. How can we solve such complex problems unless the whole sociocultural system is changed? What practical measures can be considered immediately?

Suggestions for change

Although the difficulties appear huge, we need to attempt changes if we are to encourage more women students to enroll. I identify three areas where we might make changes: a review of the OUT teaching and learning system; a reexamination of the financial requirements; and a reassessment of the OUT's position with regard to female students.

First, there is much we OUT staff could do to ensure that the pedagogical system in use at OUT is supportive of women's circumstances. The major issues are the time requirements at present, the extensive use of study centers for reference materials, tutorials and examinations, and the design of the course materials. We could begin by assessing how realistic the present course and examination timelines are given female students' life role demands, and when they apply, women need to be made aware of what is expected of them. Then we need to ensure that the study materials are delivered before the course begins to give the women maximum time for study. And to help them use their time most effectively, we could provide more advice and suggest strategies for studying. Developing more realistic deadlines and providing the means for them to study effectively would do much to help ease women's stress.

The present OUT system of frequent visits to study centers for tutoring and regional centers for examinations and practicals needs to be reassessed. Course designers need to be made aware that female learners do not have easy and frequent access to libraries or the freedom or resources to travel to study centers. One alternative would be to develop self-contained study and evaluation materials. This would remove the need for the women to obtain regular permission to travel to the study centers and, in my estimation, greatly increase the likelihood of women enrolling with the OUT. Another alternative would be to provide woman-friendly, clean, and safe hostel accommodation in the regional centers, which would help more women gain access to OUT programs.

Second, OUT operational procedures have exacerbated the female students' financial difficulties. A solution offered by several women was for the government to provide full tuition bursaries and for the OUT to remove the regional center food and accommodation expenses. They believed that the present structure reflected the dominant male view and was a deliberate attempt to stop women from obtaining a university education. As one put it:

> Most Tanzanian men know the culture, and the male domination of the woman: that not many women will be allowed by their husbands to attend university studies, demanding so much money and putting wives in guest houses/hotels in towns for so many days.

They also blamed the government, arguing that it knew the average income of employed women when the costs for study with the OUT were set and should therefore have known that most women learners in low-paying jobs would be at a disadvantage.

Third, as well as addressing the discrimination embedded in its pedagogical and financial systems, the OUT could be more active in modeling its desire to provide equal educational opportunities by adopting a different standard for women's participation in its activities. It could involve more women in its planning and administration to ensure that decisions include gender analysis. One OUT senator and a councillor since the university's inception who has consistently tried to address the systemic issues blocking women's academic success expressed her frustration with the system: "Women have been raising this matter, over, and over and over and over." She went on to explain that at last they have convinced the administration to include a gender analysis when they have supplied any statistics. She continued:

> We have proposed many ways of reaching women, and really giving the idea of open learning as the way for women and girls to catch-up with their education. ... But we have failed very much. We have paid lip service more than really do something tangible.

One reason for the difficulties and frustrations of female academics such as this councillor and myself is that many of our male colleagues have no conception of the realities of OUT women students' lives. For example, a senior colleague, when explaining what he considered to be the major factors preventing many women from enrolling with the OUT, said:

> The distance education program is designed for those who are ready to push themselves rather than to be pushed by somebody. So our [OUT] responsibility is to provide the enabling environment and it is for the clientele to take the advantage of the environment that is provided. ... So the responsibility rests on the target groups. The best we [OUT] could do within the system would be to raise consciousness, awareness of the existence of such programs, the levels, the potential, and maybe the benefits of such programs.

This statement takes the predominant view that the OUT need only offer the service: it is up to the women to apply. No consideration is given to whether they are free to make this choice. The Forum for African Women Educationalists argues that in

> planning for development of any project, it is necessary that there be equal participation of the decision making bodies, in this case, Tanzanian men and women be equally represented if the project is to benefit all parties, thus be gender-free/not lopsided.
>
> (1998: 38–40)

One beginning student explained it well:

> By their nature, men and women are different although they are all human beings; just as mango trees and orange trees are different, although they are all fruit trees. As such, it is not easy for mango trees to take nutrients from the soil to give to orange trees. In the same vein, it is not easy for men to plan developments that fit women although they are all human beings.

I believe that if enough women had taken part in the early planning of the development of the OUT, the issues involving women's participation would have been raised more clearly, with the result that relevant services would have been improved and higher participation rates achieved. At present all senior administrative staff are men. This situation needs to be remedied.

Because the OUT acknowledges the low numbers of women applicants, it has taken some steps to understand the underlying reasons. One step was to create the position of Dean of Students, to be held by a woman, because as the administrative head of student matters a woman would more easily understand the problems of female students and be better able to guide and encourage them. In addition, the OUT and the government have made some efforts to obtain financial aid for female students' tuition fees, although the amounts are small (OUT 2000).

Much work remains to be done. To address the issues related to setting policy for increased access and sustained academic success, for the effective use of various learning technologies, and for raising participation rates above the current 12 percent, we need a systemic review of educational assumptions and processes and increased staff development. If the operational services are adjusted, fees and regional center costs taken care of, and study materials and examinations made self-contained and home-delivered, then it would be a mark of our success as OUT staff if on the OUT's tenth anniversary in 2005 the participation rates for women were 50 percent and this larger group of women students were working with their new student colleagues to help them learn distance education study techniques.

Suggestions

1   In identifying why there is such a low participation rate for women and what might be done to resolve these difficulties, I found it essential to talk to students and former students. I suggest the same route for others. The women's stories of how they had tried to overcome the barriers in their path were heartwarming and saddening. They fueled my persistence to try to ensure that we did not make the same mistakes with other students.

2   It is easy to become overwhelmed when it seems that all the sociocultural and economic structures are designed to keep women from active participation. I found it helpful to identify arenas where I could focus my concerns. First, at the government level, it is important to share the women's experiences in ways that might help bring about policy changes. For me, the financial difficulties for women is one area where the government might be made aware of how its policy in setting OUT fees effectively reduces the likelihood of participation for many women in low-paying jobs.

3   At the institutional level, I asked what we as an institution might do within these barriers (such as not forcing women to choose between disobeying their husbands or participating at a study center) to enhance the learning opportunities for women students.

4   It is also important that we model what we hope society will adopt: equality of participation. Hence at the staff level, I think workshops that sensitize staff to these unique-to-women issues and structural changes that accord women visible participation through all levels of the organization are ways to "walk our talk" of wanting full participation of women students.

References

Forum for African Women Educationalists (1998) *Gender Analysis for Educational Policy Making*. Nairobi: Author.

Mbughuni, P. (1994) "Gender and Poverty Alleviation in Tanzania. Recent Research Issues," in M.S.D. Bagachwa (ed.) *Poverty Alleviation in Tanzania. Recent Research Issues*. Dar es Salaam: Dar es Salaam University Press.

Ministry of Science, Technology and Higher Education (1999) *Some Basic Statistics on Higher Learning Institutions in Tanzania 1994/5–1998/99*. Dar es Salaam: Dar es Salaam University Printers.

Mkapa, B. (1996) *Opening Speech on the Occasion for Inauguration of Additional Work Space for the Open University of Tanzania at TRDO Premises*. Dar es Salaam: Open University of Tanzania.

Mmari, G.R.V. (1997) "Putting Knowledge to Use in the Information Age," *HURIA, Journal of the Open University of Tanzania*, 1, 2, 112.

Open University of Tanzania (OUT) (2000) *Prospectus*, Dar es Salaam: Kiuta Printers.

Stambach, A. (2000) *Lessons from Mount Kilimanjaro: Schooling, Community, and Gender in East Africa*. New York: Routledge.

Synder, M. and Tadesse, M. (1995) *African Women's Development: A History*. London: Zed Books.

Part 4

Quality issues

The first three chapters discuss issues in the evaluation of course and program design and implementation, because evaluation is essential to acquiring accurate information for enhancing programs and setting policy. Charlotte Gunawardena reflects on the course of her research that has been driven by her continuing interest in evaluating online learning and her own experience with teaching online. Mary Thorpe combines her personal research interest in evaluation and her lengthy experience in her institutional evaluative role to review recurrent and generic issues of evaluation. Christine von Prümmer and Ute Rossié, as full-time institutional researchers, focus on the complex evaluative questions that need to be asked if an institution is serious about the impact of gender on technologically mediated learning. In the concluding chapter, Liz Burge draws together themes and ideas from all the chapter authors to provide a synthesis of their stated challenges in using learning technologies and a concise summary of their guidelines for informed – but not always easy – practice.

11 Reflections on evaluating online learning and teaching

Charlotte N. Gunawardena

Introduction

As electronic knowledge networks transform the way we teach and learn, we need to develop appropriate methodologies and tools for evaluating online learning. The key features of online learning – time-independence, text format, computer mediation, multiple threads of conversation, and fluid participation patterns – pose particular kinds of challenge. Online learning designs, in my experience at least, tend to be based on constructivist and learner-centered principles that act to increase learners' control, facilitate the sharing of multiple perspectives, and emphasize encouraging individual learners to create their own meaning (Jonassen *et al.* 1995; Wilson and Lowry 2001). Achieving behavioral objectives with the same stated outcome for all learners is not the goal of many online learning projects. Traditional evaluation methods used to evaluate learning within the four walls of a classroom do not transfer well to the online context. Therefore, evaluators need to understand the inherent distinguishing features of online activity and its social and ecological structure so that they may adopt new principles appropriate for evaluating learning.

In this chapter I discuss my 10 years of evaluation activities relating to online learning experiences, which range from setting up online networks for social interaction, facilitating collaborative learning experiences among graduate students in several universities, moderating worldwide online professional development activities, and teaching entirely online. Most of this experience relates to my role as a professor at the University of New Mexico (UNM) where I teach graduate level courses in distance education and educational telecommunications. I wish to acknowledge here the valuable lessons learned from many students and colleagues who have collaborated with me and helped develop my understanding of how learning occurs in online networks. For me the greatest value of online learning lies in the concept of *networked learning*, that is, the opportunity to engage in collaborative, reflective learning for an extended period with individuals who may be thousands of miles apart and in different time zones. As I study online learning, I am more interested in discovering the *process* of learning rather than the *product*, that is, how did this specific online group share multiple perspectives, negotiate meaning, and come to new understandings? And how did individual participants in this group change their own perceptions as a result of this group process? One of the difficulties I have experienced as a practitioner is assigning individual worth to collaborative group learning processes when institutional policies often require assessment of individual learning.

Formal definitions and methodologies of evaluation abound (Guba and Lincoln 1981; Patton 1986; Preskill and Torres 1999). I define *evaluation* as a purposeful and systematic inquiry that includes collecting, analyzing, and reporting data relating to the appropriateness, efficiency, effectiveness, value, and outcomes of a process, product, or program. My evaluation plans include both evaluation and research questions. Evaluation questions center on the value or outcomes of a program; research questions focus on why I saw certain outcomes. Because online learning is a complex activity, we should not limit evaluation to a single question or method. This chapter shows the range of questions I have asked and the methods used to find some answers. The questions refer to participation, learners' satisfaction levels, knowledge construction, and instructors' experiences.

How may we describe participation?

The term *participation* here refers to message frequency, interaction patterns, and group dynamics. Participation analysis techniques examine the capacity of a conference to engage members and reveal comparative patterns of participation among learners from varying backgrounds. Relevant questions here relating to student participation and interaction patterns include:

1   Who were the participants, and what were their response obligations in relation to the required online tasks?
2   Was the computer conference sufficiently interesting and worthwhile that people became and remained involved?
3   How can we describe the pattern of online interactions and group dynamics?

An evaluation tool that I have found useful is the interaction analysis model (Levin *et al.* 1990). Its four dimensions of analysis – participant structures, intermessage reference, message act, and message flow – keep my evaluator's eyes on the broad view of the network organization and activities. We used this model to evaluate a peer support network for UNM medical students who needed a social and psychological support network while they worked with preceptors in isolated rural communities in New Mexico (Gunawardena *et al.* 1991). The participant structures analysis indicated that the use of the system was voluntary, no assignments were posted, and no expected level of use was required. The intermessage reference analysis resulted in a message map stretching to several sheets of pasted paper with lines drawn in every direction showing the relationship between messages. We wondered whether our analysis was worth the effort, but it showed that messages referenced three and four times had contained content associated with solving a puzzle or playing a game. This result suggested to us that when there was a common goal – even in a network set up mainly for social interaction – more participants were likely to interact. Our analysis also indicated that making participants comfortable with the use of the technical system early led to immediate and continued use of the system. Message act analysis revealed that the medical students interacted in a "thread" pattern rather than a "star" pattern, most probably because no specific discussion topics were introduced. There were no persons online holding power (e.g., a faculty member who would have evaluated a message or instructed participants to discuss a particular topic). We found the Levin *et al.* (1990) model insufficient for exploring the nature of the interactions. In such a quantitative analysis of messages, no provision was made for addressing the content of interactions, a shortcoming recognized by the authors themselves. We (Gunawardena *et al.* 1991) therefore suggest expanding the Levin *et al.* model to include content analysis based on qualitative research techniques as part of message act analysis. Using content analysis, we were able to get at the flavor of the online social network and understand the kinds of activity medical students engaged in in their respective rural communities. Message flow analysis revealed that students took seven weeks to become comfortable with the system as a communications tool, but after that they were consistent users until two weeks before the end of the preceptorship. In reflecting later on our use of this model, we found that, although it is a good starting point for obtaining a broad picture of the network group, its activities, and interaction, it has limits. We would be better served with an evaluation model that helped us gather other data such as unsolicited and solicited participants' reactions online and instructors' and students' perspectives on interaction.

Are learners satisfied?

To find out whether learners are satisfied, I most often use online surveys, paper-and-pencil surveys, and participants' reactions posted online in a designated conference area. Another important source of data is the mass of unsolicited comments that appear in conference transcripts. Structured survey questions help gain an overall view of students' reactions to the conference and their satisfaction. It is also possible to obtain more in-depth data on selected open-ended questions. Needs assessment surveys administered before the start of a computer conference enable us to gain a picture of learners' characteristics so that the conference and support system can be designed to meet their needs and skills. The survey is an easy means of obtaining data when students are scattered across geographic distance.

Analysis of survey data has taken many forms depending on the questions being asked.

In the study with medical students described above (Gunawardena *et al.* 1991), we used a structured questionnaire to assess students' reactions to the use of computer-mediated communications as a peer support network. It was generally perceived to be a great success, but it also emerged that unlike their male colleagues, female students considered social and academic interaction with their peers through e-mail to be important. We missed the opportunity to follow this up with qualitative interviews. Using survey data and quantitative analysis, I have explored in two studies (Gunawardena and Zittle 1997; Gunawardena and Duphorne 2000) answers to the question: What are the variables that can predict student satisfaction in online learning networks? Both studies used survey data from the interuniversity GlobalEd online conference that enabled 50 graduate students from five universities to discuss research and experience distance education by using computer-mediated communication (CMC). For the 1997 study we used eight process variables: social presence, active participation, attitude toward CMC, barriers to participation (including technical problems and lack of access), confidence in mastering the CMC system, perception of having an equal opportunity to participate, adequate training in CMC at the participant's site, and technical skills and experience in using CMC. Our stepwise regression analysis converged on a three-predictor model revealing that social presence, student perception of having equal opportunity to participate in the conference, and proficiency in technical skills accounted for about 68 percent of the explained variance. Social presence alone contributed about 60 percent of this variance, suggesting that this may be a strong predictor of satisfaction. Although we cannot generalize these results because of sample selection and size, the results suggest that social presence alone is a strong predictor of satisfaction in a text-based computer conference. This finding supports earlier research that showed that the relational or social aspect of CMC is an important element that contributes to the overall satisfaction of task-oriented or academic computer conferences (Walther 1992; Baym 1995). Our later study (Gunawardena and Duphorne 2000) explored predictors of learner satisfaction in a computer conference, basing the analysis on the Adult Distance Study Through Computer Conferencing (ADSCC) model developed by Eastmond (1994) using grounded theory approaches. Eastmond identified three sequential influencers of students' study experiences: readiness to study, online features, and learning approaches. I used these three factors to see which would best predict student satisfaction with an online conference. I found that, although 56 percent of the variance is accounted for by these three factors, the online features was the best predictor, with 28 percent of the variance.

Reflecting on the various quantitative analyses I have carried out, I think that their strengths lie in their ability to show salient differences in student characteristics or process variables as they relate to learners' satisfaction. One of the shortcomings of such analyses, however, is my inability to explain the reasons for the significant differences observed, so I need to use qualitative analyses of open-ended questions or interviews. A related problem with quantitative analysis (when applied to online contexts) is the typical small sample size in many conferences and the problems related to sample selection: random sampling is difficult in distance education contexts because distance students often select the distance education option themselves. Quantitative analyses should be performed only when there is an adequate sample size to study the variables of interest. Qualitative data used in conjunction with quantitative data can usually explain the significant differences found. Therefore, I advocate a mixed methodology approach (Tashakkori and Teddlie 1998).

How do learners experience online activity?

How does the individual learner make sense of the computer conference? What is he or she learning? These questions are more difficult to answer if we subscribe to a constructivist view of learning where the individual learner is expected to use various contextual resources and guidance to construct her or his own conceptual frameworks. Traditional methods of measuring learning using pre- and posttests will not work well in this context because learning occurs in many different forms and is not limited to learning the content or subject under study.

I continue to be interested in examining evaluation questions related to learning from two perspectives: What did participants learn about the subject that was discussed? And what did they learn about the medium of computer conferencing and its influence on the learning process? One method is to analyze the computer transcript because it affords an unobtrusive and fairly accurate means of gauging whether participants learned during the conference. If I look carefully at the transcript, I can decipher unsolicited and/or thinking-aloud comments that refer to individual learning. Evaluation data on the learners' actual learning experiences can also be collected by asking participants directly what they learned, either through open-ended questions in questionnaires or individual interviews (via e-mail, telephone, or face to face), asking them to discuss their learning in a special conference space, or asking online a general question such as "What did you think about this computer conferencing experience?" The use of qualitative in-depth interviews and triangulated data analysis methods gives us rich data about how learners themselves understand and articulate the complexities of their online learning experience (Burge 1994; Eastmond 1994). Bullen (1998) used a case study approach with both quantitative and qualitative data to identify the factors most often cited by students as either facilitating or inhibiting their participation and critical thinking in online discussions.

To understand the many forms of learning that occur in online courses, I have often asked students to keep weekly journals documenting all aspects of their learning. Although they gave me a unique perspective of each individual's learning process, using journals is problematic: students may be reluctant to disclose their own learning experiences, and university ethics review committees are concerned about violating students' privacy. Other techniques include asking students to critique their online learning experiences and to apply and transfer what they have learned from the online conference to developing a new online conference design. I have learned that qualitative approaches work better than quantitative methods in gaining understanding of how individual students believe they learn in online contexts.

How is knowledge constructed in social negotiation?

The question of how knowledge is constructed is grounded in social constructivist theory, which posits that knowledge is constructed through social interaction and collaboration with others (Vygotsky 1978). To address this question adequately, I believe we must engage in the challenging task of content analysis or interaction analysis of computer transcripts using qualitative research techniques. I have relied earlier on interaction analysis to find answers about knowledge construction, and our efforts led ultimately to the development of an interaction analysis model for examining social construction of knowledge in online learning networks (Gunawardena *et al.* 1997). The development of the interaction analysis model started when we began to analyze the transcripts of a global online debate we had conducted as an adult professional development experience involving 54 volunteers from several countries who were either practicing professionals or graduate students in distance education. We began our thinking with the question "Was knowledge constructed within the group by means of the exchanges among participants?" and chose Henri's (1992) interaction analysis model as the most promising starting point. It soon became clear that three aspects of Henri's model – its basis in a teacher-centered instructional paradigm, its distinction between the cognitive and the metacognitive dimensions, and its treatment of the concept of interaction – were not suitable for our purposes. We needed to develop a new definition of interaction for the online context if we were to examine the process of social negotiation of knowledge. We believe the metaphor of a patchwork quilt may be used to describe the process of shared construction of knowledge. A quilt block is built up by the quilter by applying small pieces of cloth one after another to form a bright and colorful pattern. The pieces of cloth represent individual online contributions, each showing its own texture and color of thought just as every scrap of fabric forms a distinctive element in the overall pattern of a quilt. The pattern may not be completed during a single conference, but individual responses can contribute to the formation of a pattern. The process by which the contributions are fitted together is interaction, broadly understood, and the pattern that emerges at the end when the entire gestalt of accumulated interaction is viewed is the newly created knowledge or meaning. Interaction is the essential process of joining the idea pieces in the co-creation of knowledge.

Based on our new definition of interaction and on grounded theory data analysis, we developed a framework of interaction analysis that is appropriate for assessing a constructivist learning experience online. The experience was analyzed for the type of cognitive activity shown in the text to have been performed by participants (questioning, clarifying, negotiating, synthesizing, etc.), the types of arguments advanced throughout the debate, the resources brought in by participants to explore and negotiate new meanings, and the evidence of changes in knowledge development as a result of interactions in the group. Using these four analysis foci, we developed an outline of the process of negotiation that appears to occur in the co-construction of knowledge. The outline led to the development of a five-phase model of the negotiation process. We believe that our model serves as a useful initial framework for analyzing the process of learning in online interactions, but further research is needed.

How do teachers experience online work?

While I was researching students' reactions to online learning, I was also engaged in teaching online. Teachers' reflections on facilitating online learning experiences provide an excellent means of engaging in practitioner evaluation and understanding the successes, frustrations, and messiness of online projects. Although we can interview teachers to collect such data, one technique that has worked well for me is to work collaboratively with colleagues who have participated in online projects to reflect on and write about our own experiences and from these derive guidelines for designing future computer conferences. The GlobalEd interuniversity computer conference, which linked graduate students in several universities in the US and Australia to participate in collaborative research, was an excellent example of such collaboration and reflection on our online teaching experiences in our own institutional contexts (Gunawardena *et al.* 1994; Rezabek *et al.* 1994; Murphy *et al.* 1995). My own experience in designing and facilitating international online learning projects has helped me learn the importance of examining cultural issues that affect online group dynamics and interactions. I began examining these issues after facilitating collaborative learning experiences between my students and graduate students at the University of Guadalajara in Mexico (Wilson *et al.* 2000).

Another useful approach is to examine the role changes and reactions that teachers experience in the online context. I discuss my own role changes and the adjustments needed to move from a teacher-centered to a learner-centered instructional paradigm when teaching online in Gunawardena (1992). Annand and Haughey (1997) describe naturalistic inquiry approaches used to examine six instructors' experiences with computer conferencing; Gibson

(2000) explores with some frankness some of her reactions as an online teacher; and Salmon (2000) provides additional evaluative commentaries from the "heat" of online action.

Final words

I wish to end this reflection about online evaluation with my list of key areas and questions to address and the best guidelines I can offer my colleagues as they plan for evaluation of online activity.

As we develop innovative designs for teaching and learning through online networks, one of the key areas to examine is the *process* of online learning. For example, how is knowledge constructed through the process of collaboration and social negotiation? What is the nature of this socially shared cognition? Another area is the relational or social nature of online networks and how this influences the online learning process. As online learning offerings expand to include diverse populations in cross-cultural and international settings, we need to understand the cultural influences that affect motivation to contribute online, approaches to learning, thought patterns, interaction, and group dynamics. A fourth area is the interplay of online learning and teaching as a dynamic system with its components pulling, tugging, and influencing each other.

The best suggestion I can offer anyone wishing to evaluate online learning and teaching is to maintain an open and inquiring mind. Avoid absolutely approaching the task with preconceived notions about the advantages of one method over another. It is crucial to ask the important questions, define them clearly, and select a combination of methods to answer them. I have found that adopting a single technique for analyzing the quality of the learning experience in online learning networks has not yielded satisfactory answers. The complex nature of online learning calls for the use of multiple methods and multiple sources of data to understand group as well as individual learning. My own future evaluation activities will, I am sure, move me on to different questions and methods and the adoption and development of new models to understand better the complex and dynamic nature of online learning and teaching.

References

Annand, D. and Haughey, M. (1997) "Instructors' Orientations Towards Computer-Mediated Learning Environments," *Journal of Distance Education*, 12, 1/2, 127–152.

Baym, N.K. (1995) "The Emergence of Community in Computer-Mediated Communication," in S.G. Jones (ed.) *Cybersociety*. Newbury Park, CA: Sage.

Bullen, M. (1998) "Participation and Critical Thinking in Online University Distance Education," *Journal of Distance Education*, 13, 2, 1–32.

Burge, E.J. (1994) "Learning in Computer Conferenced Contexts: The Learners' Perspective," *Journal of Distance Education*, 9, 1, 19–43.

Eastmond, D.V. (1994) "Adult Distance Study Through Computer Conferencing," *Distance Education*, 15, 1, 128–152.

Gibson, C.C. (2000) "The Ultimate Disorienting Dilemma: The Online Learning Community," in T. Evans and D. Nation (eds) *Changing University Teaching: Reflections on Creating Educational Technologies*. London: Kogan Page.

Guba, E.G. and Lincoln, Y.S. (1981) *Effective Evaluation*. San Francisco, CA: Jossey-Bass.

Gunawardena, C.N. (1992) "Changing Faculty Roles for Audiographics and Online Teaching," *American Journal of Distance Education*, 6, 3, 58–71.

Gunawardena, C.N., Campbell Gibson, C., Cochenour, J.J., Dean, T., Dillon, C.L., Hessmiller, R., Murphy, K., Rezabek, L.L., and Saba, F. (1994) "Multiple Perspectives on Implementing Inter-University Computer Conferencing," in *Proceedings of the Distance Learning Research Conference*. College Station, TX: Texas A&M University, Department of Educational Human Resource Development.

Gunawardena, C.N. and Duphorne, P.L. (2000) "Predictors of Learner Satisfaction in an Academic Computer Conference," *Distance Education*, 21, 1, 101–117.

Gunawardena, C.N., Gittinger Jr., J.D., and Dvorak, L.P. (1991) "The Design, Implementation and Evaluation of a Computer-Mediated Communication Support System for Medical Students," in *Proceedings of the Seventh Annual Conference on Distance Teaching and Learning*. Madison, WI: University of Wisconsin-Madison.

Gunawardena, C.N., Lowe, C.A., and Anderson, T. (1997) "Analysis of a Global Online Debate and the Development of an Interaction Analysis Model for Examining Social Construction of Knowledge in Computer Conferencing," *Journal of Educational Computing Research*, 17, 4, 395–429.

Gunawardena, C.N. and Zittle, F. (1997) "Social Presence as a Predictor of Satisfaction Within a Computer Mediated Conferencing Environment," *American Journal of Distance Education*, 11, 3, 8–25.

Henri, F. (1992) "Computer Conferencing and Content Analysis," in A.R. Kaye (ed.) *Collaborative Learning Through Computer Conferencing: The Najaden Papers*. Berlin, New York: Springer-Verlag.

Jonassen, D., Davidson, M., Collins, M., Campbell, J., and Haag, B. (1995) "Constructivism and Computer-Mediated Communication in Distance Education," *American Journal of Distance Education*, 9, 2, 7–26.

Levin, J.A., Kim, H., and Riel, M.M. (1990) "Analyzing Instructional Interactions on Electronic Message Networks," in L. Harasim (ed.) *Online Education*. New York: Praeger.

Murphy, K., Boyce, M., Cochenour, J., Dean, T., Dillon, C., Gibson, C., Gunawardena, C., and Rezabek, L.L. (1995) "Computer-Mediated Communications in a Collaborative Learning Environment: The GlobalEd Project," in D. Sewart (ed.) *One World Many Voices: Quality in Open and Distance Learning*. Birmingham: Open University.

Patton, M.Q. (1986) *Utilization-Focused Evaluation*. Newbury Park, CA: Sage.

Preskill, H. and Torres, R.T. (1999) *Evaluative Inquiry for Learning in Organizations*. Thousand Oaks, CA: Sage.

Rezabek, L.L., Boyce, M., Cochenour, J., Dean, T., Dillon, C., Campbell Gibson, C., Gunawardena, C.N., Hessmiller, R., Murphy, K., Saba, F., and Weibel, K. (1994) "CMC as Learner-Centered Instruction: Lessons from GLOBALED '93," in *Proceedings of the Tenth Annual Conference on Distance Teaching and Learning*. Madison, WI: University of Wisconsin-Madison.

Salmon, G. (2000) *E-Moderating: The Key to Teaching and Learning Online*. London: Kogan Page.

Tashakkori, A. and Teddlie, C. (1998) *Mixed Methodology: Combining Qualitative and Quantitative Approaches*. Thousand Oaks, CA: Sage.

Vygotsky, L. (1978) *Mind in Society: The Development of Higher Psychological Processes*. Cambridge, MA: Harvard University Press.

Walther, J.B. (1992) "Interpersonal Effects in Computer-Mediated Interaction: A Relational Perspective," *Communication Research*, 19, 1, 52–90.

Wilson, B. and Lowry, M. (2001) "Constructivist Learning on the Web," in E.J. Burge (ed.) *The Strategic Use of Learning Technologies, New Directions for Adult and Continuing Education No. 88*. San Francisco, CA: Jossey-Bass.

Wilson, P.L., Gunawardena, C.N., and Nolla, A.C. (2000) "Cultural Factors Influencing Online Interaction and Group Dynamics," in *Proceedings of the 16th Annual Conference on Distance Teaching and Learning*. Madison, WI: University of Wisconsin-Madison.

12 Evaluating the use of learning technologies

Mary Thorpe

Professional identities develop and change with one's role, but for me evaluation has always been part of what I do as a distance educator. In the early 1990s I published a book on evaluating open and distance learning that was also about practitioner evaluation (Thorpe 1993). I wished to draw together and reflect on a period of intensive work with colleagues in the regional system of the Open University in the United Kingdom (OUUK), evaluating the role of tutors and others involved in supporting learners. Although I had already discovered many of the key truths about evaluation by that stage, I have now been for six years in the different position of Director of the Institute of Educational Technology (IET) at the OUUK (http://iet.open.ac.uk), where evaluation is the sole focus of a large group of professional survey researchers and academics. In many ways, all the personal discoveries I made earlier through direct experience as a practitioner-researcher are still relevant. Here are some key learnings: evaluators are often at risk of drowning under the weight of their own data; questionnaires are always improved by piloting; and writing the report always takes longer than anticipated.

This chapter offers me the luxury of a personal reflection on the current state of evaluation in the light of the explosion of information communication technologies (ICTs) across all sectors of provision, campus-based no less than open and distance learning (ODL). These learning technologies are not just the latest version of ODL: they are revolutionizing how we teach and learn. They also represent a renaissance for evaluation and for the evaluator who is now asked to advise inexperienced others in how to evaluate innovative use of learning technology. Across the world, educators, many of whom are inexperienced users of learning technologies, are encouraged to innovate and report the results. These educators recognize that evaluation is necessary, but may lack the required skills to perform it. For example, a new organization to encourage ICT development among higher education teachers was established in the UK after the MacFarlane report (Committee of Scottish University Principals 1992) proposed increased use of learning technologies. The new Association for Learning Technology publishes newsletters and a journal, which carry regular reports of experience and sometimes formal evaluations of practice in using learning technologies in a variety of institutions (http://www.warwick.ac.uk/alt-E/).

Defining evaluation

The literature on evaluation offers much room for debate about its function and rationale. For our purposes a working definition suffices: evaluation is the collection, analysis, and interpretation of evidence about the effects and outcomes of a selected activity or form of provision. It includes both intended and unintended outcomes and should support the making of judgments about the activity or the provision.

I prefer to emphasize evaluation as a public activity. Many activities, notably management, involve making judgments about effectiveness, but they do not thereby become evaluation. Evaluation should be deliberate and open to inspection. Although the results may never be published, they should be planned and justifiable to others. What distinguishes evaluation from other related activities is not just that judgments are made, but that they are seen to be made and on the basis of certain claims to evidence. It follows that our evidence should bear inspection by a disinterested observer. Fortunately, many guides and textbooks on evaluation methods are available to help the practitioner meet this challenge.

Although my own role has changed, I can look back over 25 years of evaluation of learning technologies and reflect on what is still relevant. I discuss here what I have learned as the key issues facing evaluators of old and new learning technologies. These issues are access and learner profiling, usability (especially in developmental testing of materials), changing roles of learners and tutors, and new opportunities created by online technology.

Access and learner profiling

Here is a complex mix. Some common technologies that support learning involve little more than putting teaching resources onto intranet sites, providing search engines for accessing Internet resources, and setting up conferencing and e-mailing. Few institutions teach wholly online, and most combine these electronic media with print, face to face, and more established technologies such as telephone, CD-ROM, radio, and television. Whatever the combination, practitioners often forget issues of access and usability.

Access and profiling are about whether learners use the course or resources as intended. We should check this before assessing the effectiveness of an innovation. Evaluation at this stage is important for coming to know the target learner group better and for developmental testing.

Learner profiling is finding out if we really know our intended learners – not just their ages and qualifications, but how and where they prefer to study, what they want from study, their longer term goals, and so on. These and many other factors play a significant part in how learners react to the opportunities we provide. For example, we assume that learners have the time available to study according to the schedules we build into our courses. But is it really possible for full-time workers, for example, to study effectively if they need to spend an hour or so searching for relevant articles? Do designers assume that they can study for three hours a session when more realistically they can spare chunks of an hour at most and use weekends to catch up where necessary? A profile of learners constructed through surveys, with perhaps some interviews, can provide a qualitative picture of the range of learner types. Woodley and Ashby (1994) provide a helpful account of how to do this.

However, most practitioners know that access to hardware and software required by their program will be an issue. Bulletin boards, for example, may be a perfect method for keeping technicians up to date with the latest techniques in their field, but as not all employers allow study in the workplace, the issue of access should be checked at an early stage.

There are many other reasons to find out about the intended users of learning technologies, and a combination of existing data and sample survey methods are the best solution. In the UK, for example, we rely on data from the Office for National Statistics (1999, 2000) about home ownership of computers and Internet access to guide general expectations about the national picture for particular socioeconomic groups. These data are updated annually and reveal how quickly ownership of technology changes. Nevertheless, we have also had to conduct regular surveys of our own students for more accurate information about how many of each faculty's learners have access at home or work.

Thus we know that ownership of computers among the general population has risen rapidly, from 26 percent of UK households in 1996–97 to 34 percent in 1998–99 (ONS, http://www.statistics.gov.uk/). However, ownership is four times higher in households headed by a professional than those headed by unskilled manual workers. Our own surveys of OUUK students show much higher ownership, from about 70 percent in the arts faculty to nearly 100 percent in the business school and technology faculties. Such findings obviously reflect the fact that we now require students to have access to computers for effective study on a growing number of our courses. However, ownership data have also influenced the decision to provide subsidized access to machines for those on low incomes and help for tutors to purchase their own machines.

Usability and developmental testing

Learning technologies typically require that systems and learning materials be designed in advance. Such design is based on assumptions about what our learners can do and how they will react to our materials. Because their learning takes place when a tutor is not there, it is vital to pilot the technology with a small number of typical learners. Developmental testing of this kind has proved its value many times over by identifying and correcting major problems that learners experience before the first full run of the program.

Without prerelease course evaluation, programs may fail not because our basic ideas were poor, but because learners could not make effective use of what we offered. Here is one example. CD-ROMs and online resources are designed by those who are familiar with screen-based design, pull-down menus, highlighting, "hot" spots, and so on. These experts are unable to put themselves in the position of a novice, so it is essential for educational designers to test their designs developmentally so that feedback from users can be used to make changes. Nielsen and Norman (www.useit.com), for example, show that most user difficulties stem from poor design, not user incompetence.

Once course materials are in use, practitioners should be able to answer the questions "Have we achieved what we set out to achieve, and why?" Evidence for some answers will be available without a specific evaluation: test results if these have been part of the program, levels of activity of the learners, comments from those tutoring or managing the program, and so on. However, this may not be enough. Learning technologies typically create changes in a number of key areas in the teaching and learning process, and these should be the focus for appropriate and planned evaluation. Let me explain.

Adding learning technologies to the resource base of learning programs may increase the study time required in two ways. First, where several media are in use, the effort of understanding what each medium carries and how best to use it may add to the total study time required. Second, these technologies typically contain optional resources, so learners may spend time learning more than they need to – or simply get hooked on an optional extra and spend longer using it than the course designers intended. Although this may not be negative in itself, the effects can be undesirable if learners fall behind in other essential areas or worry about whether they are learning the "right things."

The issue of workload has always been important, because distance learners are usually part time and fit study in with the other demands of adult life. A key evaluation issue in the 1970s, for example, was learning how to structure course resources and assessment so that learners could pace themselves effectively. We learned that dropout rates would rise if we allowed a sudden increase in the level of difficulty of course material or in the amount of work required. Such action would be the "last straw" for learners who were unsure of themselves or their ability to complete the course. However, by the 1990s, workload had lost out to other issues such as evaluation of specific innovative course elements, CD-ROMs, and computer-mediated communication (CMC) in particular. Now workload has regained its importance because of an increase in dropout rates.

Recent surveys of OUUK learners who drop out have produced the same findings year after year. Underestimating the time required for study, together with the competing demands on their time from home and work, are the reasons most people give for giving up. We are exploring whether there is a connection between this issue of time and time pressure and the increasing number of media in our courses. We now offer our students an enriched, but more complex set of resources and we risk that this media mix may fragment students' attentions and demand more study time even for keeping track of the learning package. So mapping learner workload has become a key issue both at the developmental testing stage and in the evaluation of courses. Early action may be necessary to reduce unacceptably high workload demands.

Changing roles

Learning technologies often change the relationship between learners and teachers and require the development of new abilities. For example, CMC enables collaborative learning, and this has been heralded as one of its chief advantages. However, it requires the design of tasks or projects that stimulate learners to engage in collaboration with their peers and also requires changes from the learners' perspectives. One of our information technology courses builds to a collaborative assignment that requires small groups to interact via e-mail and conferencing (Thorpe 1998). Individual learners must schedule their time so as to be available for the defined period of collaboration. This requires a new effort of personal time management and a willingness to take time from competing claims during that period: family holidays, work demands, and so on. Here is a real change for many learners who were used to the autonomy in learning typically offered in distance modes.

Similarly, teachers must play the roles of facilitator, learning manager, resource specialist, and so on. Text-based distance education long ago demonstrated the need for such pedagogical shifts. The newer learning technologies intensify the need and call for new skills and orientations. An interesting outcome of our uses of CMC, for example, has been the recognition that facilitation of online learning requires different skills from those of the conventional distance education tutor. Evaluation is being used here to explore what makes for the most effective online support for learners. Issues being explored are the amount and quality of interaction between learners and tutors, whether the tutor was able to foster an active group process, and the degree to which learners felt their needs were met.

New opportunities and methods

The new learning technologies generate new versions of old issues, but also create completely new opportunities for evaluation. Some examples of these new opportunities are interesting in terms of both the content and the methods of evaluation.

Take, for example, the traditional print-based distance education course. This is a relatively fixed product, with few changes from year to year. A great potential advantage of Web-based media is that they can be changed relatively easily. Whereas the aim for print-based materials was to get a course right first time, the new technologies enable a more rapid response to learner needs and content updating. This leads to regular surveys of learners so that preferences can be incorporated in the next year's changes. Courses are now seen as changing regularly, evolving from year to year. For example, the use of automated collation of relevant threads from the conferences of earlier presentations of the same course was introduced to a creative management course at the OUUK. The software operated as a virtual participant in the conferences throughout the course, allowing students to read relevant material from the previous year's students and helping them resolve questions they might have. The value of such software is that it might reduce the burden on tutors of responding to common queries and concerns (Masterton 2000). Surveys of users showed that the device could be improved in a number of ways, particularly by allowing students to ask questions via private e-mail rather than the conference, thus reducing the traffic on the conference. Even the name of the virtual participant (Uncle Bulgaria) was found to put some students off, so the developers surveyed users to check for other unexpected negative reactions so they could make changes accordingly.

The new evaluation methods becoming available are a result of the online contact we can now have with our learners. It is easier to tell them what evaluation data we require and why. A general message can be sent to all students at the start of a course explaining not only its aims, but also how those aims will be evaluated. Regular requests for feedback can be mailed to participants at the end of key sections of a course, and evidence of effectiveness can in theory be available in a matter of days. Thus a rich source of data about learners' reactions from start to finish of their learning is provided by evaluation activities built into the course.

Online delivery also offers much easier access to learners for purposes of small-scale and qualitative studies. An interview can be carried out online in the form of structured question-and-answer sessions, thus avoiding the time-consuming routine of arranging interview times, travel, and transcription of interviews. By printing out the responses of interviewees, the practitioner has a record from which to carry out content analysis and use verbatim quotations, with, of course, the permission of the interviewee.

CMC does, of course, offer a quite new resource for the evaluator: a permanent record of the transactions of the whole course, which we can retain and analyze to evaluate the effectiveness with which the learning technologies have been used. Many of the early accounts of CMC relied on the evidence of these online conversations as raw material for understanding the strengths and challenges of the new technologies in action. However, learners have understandably become sensitive to their words being used out of context. Just as conventional evaluators attempt to work within a code of ethics – such as that of the British Educational Research Association – so all who have access to the content of learner conferences and e-mails (e.g., learners, tutors, and researchers) should agree in advance on proper conventions regarding who may use their words and under what conditions.

Why evaluate?

In preparing my book on evaluation (Thorpe 1993), I had to think hard about why practitioners would want to do evaluation. Some reasons are obvious, but not compelling. We ought, for example, to evaluate the effectiveness of innovative teaching if only in the interests of our learners. Improvements are so often required, however well planned our courses. However, regardless of the desirability of evaluation, it never reduces the practitioner's workload. So why do it? My answer, then as now, is that it never fails to make life more interesting. It can sometimes vindicate one's personal beliefs, but just as often it can challenge them. One final example: I spent several years working with a technology course team on strategies for encouraging learners to reflect on *how* they were learning and how they might improve their learning abilities. We built reflective elements into the assignments that tutors marked. When I evaluated the first two years of tutor marking of these elements, I was surprised to find that little use had been made by either students or tutors of the material on learning skills. However, this increased noticeably in the second year after the course team added more specific guidance for both learners and tutors. But the first year, when the guidance was less explicit, showed that learners found it easier to reflect on how they had done their assignment than on *how well* they had achieved the goals of the assignment. Setting and applying criteria for their own work had proved more challenging. This result helped us see that reflection on learning has different aspects and demands that in turn call for different approaches from the course team and tutors. Had we not evaluated the differences between performance in these two years, we could not have developed these and many other insights into how reflection works for our learners and how it might be developed (Thorpe 2000).

In these challenging times of learning technologies, there seems less need to find reasons why practitioners should evaluate their teaching. For many the problem is not motivation, but finding the time. My advice is to take the long view. Trying to find out about everything at once incurs the risk of being overwhelmed by too much data, which becomes a barrier in itself. Decide on some priority area, or get a quick overview of general reactions on the first attempt. Plan to follow up with another study, perhaps repeating the first, but exploring in more depth a particular area that looks promising or problematic. Be sure to report on each stage. The benefit of each evaluation activity will increase, because the results at each stage together with the comparison with prior stages provide an in-depth understanding of issues. This strategy serves much better than a "big-bang" approach where one tries to do too much at once and loses enthusiasm in the work overload.

Guidelines and models for practitioners

Increased use of learning technologies encourages evaluators not only to publish the results of studies of innovations in use, but also to provide frameworks and guides to methods, which can be adapted by practitioners to their local context. Several authors have emphasized the importance of the learning context and the need to explore evidence of the outcomes of an innovation in use (Oliver 1998). I agree that it is rarely possible to answer the question of whether an example of learning technology is a better way of teaching. So often the technology changes not only how, but what is taught and learned (Jones *et al.* 1998).

Draper and Brown (1998) also identify problems with whether learning technologies are better than what went before. They argue that it is rarely possible to compare matched groups where one group experiences the innovation while the other does not. Not only is it unethical to withhold improved resources from learners, but in many contexts there is little possibility of true control. Learners may give their friends access to the materials, and the outcomes of testing measure the results of many variables in addition to the innovation itself, such as differences between tutor and learner interactions, whether learners study full or part time, and so on.

Accordingly, evaluations should focus on issues that can be fruitfully explored such as identifying the outcomes of an innovation and exploring how these outcomes come about. Practitioners are in a strong position to carry out this kind of approach, particularly if they can work collaboratively with others who are further from the innovation. It can be particularly helpful to work with an evaluation professional, and groups of practitioners working together can provide a helpful route to objectivity and clear communication of findings. Such groups should help to identify unexpected as well as expected outcomes. Many evaluations of learning technology cannot demonstrate that students do significantly better in examinations, for example, but they may show improvements in motivation or enjoyment. It is important to capture the affective as well as the cognitive side of learning.

Many practitioners think first of carrying out a sample survey using structured questionnaires. Surveys and quantitative data have a key role, but can only be used effectively if the issues and learners' perceptions are well understood. So it can be productive to carry out qualitative interviews first, and then follow up with a survey if necessary. Learners should feel comfortable with the interviewers and be able to offer their views honestly. Younger learners may be more prepared to be open about their reactions with their peers than with their tutors, so it may be desirable to recruit and train peers to conduct interviews: it is easier to be honest with a disinterested observer than with the course designer.

Suggestions

1 Learner profiling helps with course planning. Use surveys and some interviews to obtain data.
2 Check learner access to technologies. Data are changing quickly, so follow national reports closely and conduct regular surveys.

3 Pilot the learning materials. Be sure to check for learners' levels of comfort with using the technology.

4 Monitor and evaluate changes in design as result of using learning technologies.

5 Student workload is a perennial issue: keep track of it.

6 Check for the different skills and roles required with use of learning technologies for learners and tutors.

7 Plan for more frequent evaluations and for different response mechanisms in online environments.

8 Work with other practitioners. Collaboration works for us too!

9 Don't forget to examine affective as well as cognitive outcomes.

10 Start small with a project that is a priority and can be clearly defined.

Now is a good time to evaluate practice. Evaluation feeds reflection, and we can benefit from being reflective practitioners. However, education has its fashions, and evaluation may seem to have less to offer in a few years' time. No matter; in my experience, evaluation leads to practice that is better informed and therefore better prepared for whatever new challenges the technology of the day presents. To take the long view again, evaluation costs money, but it does pay back in evidence and insights about learning. It is a wise practitioner who always makes time for evaluation – whatever the fashions of the day.

References

Committee of Scottish University Principals (1992) *Teaching and Learning in an Expanding Higher Education System* (MacFarlane Report). Edinburgh: Scottish Centrally Funded Colleges.

Draper, S.W. and Brown, M.I. (1998) "Evaluating Remote Collaborative Tutorial Teaching in MANTCHI," in M. Oliver (ed.) *Innovation in the Evaluation of Learning Technology*. London: University of North London, Learning and Teaching Innovation and Development.

Jones, A., Scanlon, E., and Blake, C. (1998) "Reflections on a Model for Evaluating Learning Technologies," in M. Oliver (ed.) *Innovation in the Evaluation of Learning Technology*. London: University of North London, Learning and Teaching Innovation and Development.

Masterton, S. (2000) "The Virtual Participant: A Tutor's Assistant for Electronic Conferencing," in M. Eisenstadt and T. Vincent (eds) *The Knowledge Web: Learning and Collaborating on the Net*. London: Kogan Page.

Office for National Statistics (1999) *Social Trends 29*. London: HMI.

Office for National Statistics (2000) *Social Trends 30*. London: HMI.

Oliver, M. (1998) (ed.) *Innovation in the Evaluation of Learning Technology*. London: University of North London, Learning and Teaching Innovation and Development.

Thorpe, M. (1993) *Evaluating Open and Distance Learning* (2nd edn). Harlow: Longman.

Thorpe, M. (1998) "Assessment and 'Third Generation' Distance Education," *Distance Education*, 19, 2, 265–286.

Thorpe, M. (2000) "Encouraging Students to Reflect as Part of the Assignment Process," *Active Learning in Higher Education*, 1, 1, 79–92.

Woodley, A. and Ashby, A. (1994) "Target Audience: Assembling a Profile of Your Learners," in F. Lockwood (ed.) *Materials Production in Open and Distance Learning*. London: Paul Chapman.

13 Gender-sensitive evaluation research

Christine von Prümmer and Ute Rossié

Introduction

We have worked as institutional researchers at the German FernUniversität or Distance University (FeU) for over 20 years. Because distance teaching and learning environments have offered few opportunities for immediate student feedback, evaluation has always been for us an integral part of the development and improvement of distance education systems and study materials. We research areas such as the goals of the institution, its target groups, issues of access, dropout and completion rates, the teaching system, communication channels, and student learning environments. We also examine organizational issues and their effects on (potential) students, study behavior, learning styles, access to technology, and expenditure of time and money. In recent years the evaluation of media and information and communication technologies (ICTs) has become an increasingly important area. In this chapter we draw on our experiences as evaluators and point to key challenges and rewards of doing feminist research in a setting that may be termed androcentric and male-dominated. We begin by discussing values as an essential characteristic of evaluation, then provide a brief list of areas where neglecting gender would be prejudicial for women working and studying in open and distance learning (ODL) contexts. We end by looking at the "virtual university."

Evaluation and values

Evaluation research deals with values expressed as yardsticks, that is, goals and values against which quality is measured (Baumgartner 1999). Evaluation does not simply study social phenomena, but offers its results to policy-makers and the interested public as information on which to base concrete decisions. In education, including distance education and the virtual campus, the results of evaluation research are used to determine the quality of teaching programs and materials, instructional design and pedagogical competence, and support services and communication channels (Holst 2000; Mason 2000; Peters and De Boer 2000; von Prümmer 1998, 2000; Wetterling and Moonen 2000). In Germany recent developments are concerned with the effectiveness and quality of higher education, and intended university reforms are officially coupled with evaluation defined as "an instrument for assuring and improving quality, an instrument that supports the academic departments in their efforts to reach – or at least to approximate – self-defined goals" (Minkwitz 2000: 12).

Evaluation in open and distance learning (ODL) uses a variety of methods to seek responses to these broad questions: What constitutes "good" distance education? How do we achieve "good" distance education? And how do we measure the quality of our distance education programs? What is considered good or bad distance education depends, of course, on the views of the teacher, learner, administrator, evaluator, or policy-maker and on the set of values, educational theories, and personal preferences on which individuals or institutions ground their work.

It follows that evaluation researchers face difficult challenges. For example, anyone who has designed, taught, and evaluated an ODL course has gained first-hand experience of the complexity of evaluation research. In our experience, it involves decisions about:

- selecting and defining the criteria to be used in the evaluation
- balancing the interests of the various parties: students, teachers, administration, funding agencies, prospective employers, and one's own as evaluators
- operationalizing the questions in order to obtain a basis for recommending decisions on course design and so forth
- presenting the data in ways that will ensure attention to it, and
- possibly rewriting the course and reevaluating it.

Evaluation examines the realization of goals and intentions – manifest or latent, consistent or contradictory – but it is not necessarily involved in defining or prioritizing those goals. Still, unless evaluators take a values-based stand, they will not be able to collect and interpret meaningful data such that the results contribute effectively to quality assurance. In our own work, we value making distance education better for our students. In cases where contradictory or conflicting interests are brought to bear on our research, we try to put the interests of the students before those of the teaching staff or administration. For example, new procedures for registering electronically for exams may be more effective and less costly for the institution, but may place more burdens on students, possibly preventing those who do not have ready access to the Internet from completing their forms in time. An evaluation of the new regulations should highlight these problems and make sure that decision-makers – who might otherwise go ahead with their plans – are made aware of the risk of losing members of their target groups.

As women working in a large-scale, single-mode distance teaching university where women are underrepresented among the academic staff and students, we are especially concerned with aspects of our distance education system and pedagogy that favor men and discriminate against women. We are concerned with identifying such aspects in order to discover how we can make the university a better place for mature female students. We measure good distance education by its sensitivity to gender issues and by its ability to provide a productive and attractive learning environment for both women and men.

Gender issues

Gender is an important category for judging the quality of provision in ODL contexts (Kirkup 1996). If gender is not seen as relevant, the system will not be equally accessible to women and men and will offer men more chances to succeed. This is the case in our own institution, for example, where we face the effects of a distance education system that does not take gender into account and in both content and delivery is aimed at a generic distance student more often typified as male than female (von Prümmer 1997, 2000).

Research specifically concerned with gender issues has been carried out in ODL institutions since the early to mid-1980s, the first international comparative studies being our joint projects in Germany and Kirkup's in the UK. So far, our research has shown five areas of concern regarding gender-related matters. The first is the proportion of women in distance education programs. In Western industrialized societies women make up at least half the student population of distant teaching universities, but the German FeU is an exception: women currently are one third of the total student population of 56,000 (von Prümmer and Rossié 2000a). The second area is gender-differentiated enrollment patterns and course choices. Even where women are adequately represented or are the majority of the total student population, enrollment statistics can reflect traditional gender-related patterns of course choice and degree programs (Kirkup and von Prümmer 1997; von Prümmer and Rossié 1987, 2000a). The third area is difference in learning styles of women and men. Repeatedly our research has confirmed feminist theories (Gilligan 1982; Thompson 1983; Belenky *et al.* 1986) that note different learning styles for women and men. At the FeU and the OUUK, more female than male distance students show interest in "support and connectedness" with other students and in interactions between students and academic staff (Kirkup and von Prümmer 1990; von Prümmer 2000; von Prümmer and Rossié 1989, 1994, 2000b). In making such demands these women are not displaying a deficit in learner autonomy and independence; they approach their studies differently from many male students, but their approach is no less valid (Hauff *et al.* 1999; Heron 1997). The fourth area of concern for evaluation is gendered learning contexts. Because of family commitments, mature women – especially mothers of small children – find it more difficult than men to organize face-to-face studying (Herbst *et al.* 1994; Lunneborg 1994). In addition, many female distance students are in full-time or part-time paid work and find it difficult to attend tutorials or study groups (Kirkup and von Prümmer 1990; von Prümmer 2000). Contrary to the belief that women in unpaid family work have time on their hands and are free to organize their schedules, the everyday lives of family women are characterized by chaos and constant interruptions and are rarely self-determined (Oakley 1974; von Prümmer 2000). The fifth and final area is gender differences in access to and use of technologies. It is often assumed that the advent of ICTs and their rapid expansion in ODL contexts will automatically reduce the importance of gender as a category in evaluation (Kirkup 1996). Our research data do not support this assumption. Rather, gender plays an important role in determining the opportunities distance students have to access and use the new learning technologies to their fullest potential (Hauff 1999; Kirkup 1999; Kirkup and von Prümmer 1997; von Prümmer 1999; von Prümmer and Rossié 2000b).

Having identified these five areas, as evaluators we face the dual task of convincing the university that research on these topics is necessary and in the interest of the institution and that gender-sensitive evaluation is a valid process. Achieving these tasks means that we must (a) be able to sell our research questions and research design on their methodological strength and predicted usefulness, (b) remain in control of the data and their interpretation, and (c) disseminate the results to those who are committed to equal opportunities and able to bring about changes.

Gender issues in access and use of ICTs

Unlike written course materials, which were delivered by mail and nearly universally accessible to FeU students, technologies require hardware, software, and operational know-how, and they involve additional costs. The use of computers as teaching tools has always been accompanied by the question of students' access to technology and the ability and willingness of students and staff to experiment with the new media. The virtual university must therefore deal with the issue of access and exclusion to a greater extent than do other paper-based distance education systems. But it gets complicated. On the one hand, empirical research has repeatedly shown the gendered nature of distance education and how different institutional systems affect the participation of women. Gender differences in students' access to and use of technologies are well documented (Kirkup 1996, 1999; von Prümmer and Rossié 1996). As ICTs replace the traditional media and access to advanced technologies becomes an essential prerequisite for studying in the virtual university, women are more likely to encounter difficulties or to be excluded unless special attention is paid to the gendered nature of the new learning technologies (Kirkup and von Prümmer 1997). On the other hand, ICTs have the potential to facilitate communication and interaction between students and between students and staff in distance education settings. They may therefore be especially attractive to female distance students who tend to prefer connected learning styles and opportunities for exchange and cooperation, and who would otherwise not have a chance to meet with other students or teachers. In the FeU we find that in certain online seminars – for example, in psychology where female students predominate – women participate extensively in discussions and news groups. A recent conference held by the Women, Work and Computerization group of the International Federation of Information Processing involved a number of researchers working on new developments in communication technologies (Balka and Smith 2000). A colleague who participated reported to us that a number of projects concerning the gender-specific usage of Internet applications confirmed parallel – and all-too-familiar – gender patterns in the virtual and real worlds (Hansen 2000). According to these studies, differences between boys/men and girls/women occurred in the following areas (cited in Balka and Smith 2000): type of applications used (study by Hapnes and Rasmussen); behavior in e-mail discussions (study by Owen); problem-solving online in groups (research by Pohl and Michaelson); navigating the Web (McDonald and Spencer); preferences in Web design (Fisher and Craig); and creating and administering a woman-friendly online environment (Richardson and French).

Evaluating learning technologies for women

The following research questions have guided our research and have arisen from data we have collected in evaluation surveys.

Are groups of potential students systematically prevented from studying because they lack the resources needed to enter and succeed in the virtual university, or because the new learning environment does not cater to their specific needs and interests? Empirical research has shown the gendered nature of distance education and the participation of women (von Prümmer 2000). It is important, therefore, to determine whether the virtual university offers the same opportunities to men and women. What measures, if any, are taken to offset differential access to and control over technologies and the exclusion from electronic environments experienced by many women (Hauff *et al.* 1999)? What resources are set aside for this purpose?

Another question relates to gender differences regarding how students approach the computer. In our surveys the women, who have many more time constraints because of their multiple commitments, tend to see technology as a tool, whereas the men often like to spend time working – or playing – with the hardware and software (von Prümmer 2000). Do the media design and pedagogy in courses recognize these differences? For example, how much emphasis is given to the software ergonomics (clarity, speed of connecting, etc.) of a learning software package as opposed to pretty pictures and stunning special effects?

Woman-friendly evaluation in the virtual university – current developments

As the FeU moves toward becoming a virtual university, the focus of our evaluation research is shifting away from traditional media and communication channels to the use of the Internet.

Our research shows interesting trends that are supported by informal reports from colleagues who teach online and that warrant further exploration. Referring to unpublished data from various evaluation studies on online seminars and interactive multimedia courses, we find some common patterns. Provided they have access to the Internet, women studying at a distance seem quite willing to enter and explore online learning environments. We have data now on the participation of students in online seminars offered by the FeU departments of education, the social sciences, and the humanities. Because these are the only degree programs where women outnumber men, more women than men participate in the online seminars, e-mail, and news groups. The proportion of female students is similar to that in the overall class enrollment and in the weekend face-to-face seminars. These findings suggest that the importance of the gender issue decreases as the use of the Web in open and distance education increases.

Doing gender-sensitive research

If we take the concept of "open" and distance learning seriously, as evaluators we cannot afford to neglect issues of equity and overt or latent discrimination. It is true that many women have discovered the Internet and its potentials. It is also true, as our research shows, that gender differences still exist with respect to access and control over resources, social division of labor and time management, learning styles, and learning environments.

A case in point is our most recent survey on computer access and use of ICTs for distance studies that was conducted in 1999 with a stratified sample of approximately 5,000 degree students (von Prümmer and Rossié 2000b). The data have proven unexpectedly topical, as the FeU is currently debating whether to introduce a policy of requiring degree students to have access to a computer and to the Internet. Our data show that over 90 percent of respondents have access to a computer that they can use for study purposes and that this proportion has increased significantly in the last few years. If the trend we have observed in our surveys throughout the 1990s continues, we can expect nearly universal computer access for German distance students in the near future. Access to the Internet, although high among the distance students who participated in our survey, is less widespread: over half the respondents (55 percent) have access privately, and just under half (49 percent) have access at work. These figures are not cumulative, as many of the students have several access routes open to them.

Although there are still differences between the students in different subject areas – people studying mathematical and technical subjects are more likely to have a computer; people studying education, social sciences, and the humanities are less well equipped – the overall results show hardly any gender differences. If anything, at 93 percent the women among our respondents had even more computer access than the men at 91 percent. This result was immediately taken by the university as showing, first, that gender has become irrelevant with regard to the new technologies and, second, that mandatory computer and Internet access would not be a problem for (prospective) students.

On a less superficial level, however, the survey data do show the usual gender-differentiated patterns where women mostly have access to only one machine, usually at home, whereas many men can also access a computer at work; have less sophisticated equipment and software, especially as far as multimedia and ICT features are concerned; face more restrictions in using the technology and have less control over the home computer, which is likely to be used by other family members; have less Internet access than men, especially at work, and must rely slightly more on the provision of the technology in study centers and other external sources; and often have less experience, less interest, and less confidence in using the multimedia and ICT features of a computer.

At the least, the data analysis suggests that adopting the new policy without further consideration of women's circumstances might create problems for female distance students. These findings were possible because our research design was explicitly gender-sensitive, or woman-friendly, and included a number of questions derived from earlier research that addressed areas where gender differences occurred regularly.

Guidelines for gender-sensitive evaluation

As evaluators with extensive experience with the distance education system and the false claims about both the gender-neutrality of online systems and their equal suitability for men and women, we believe that more questions need to be asked.

1   *What resources are required?* It is clear that the participants in online seminars must own, or have unrestricted access to, a well-equipped personal computer that they can use for their studies and an affordable Internet service provider with enough lines to guarantee a reliable and fast connection. They must also have the necessary hardware and software – for example, video capability, a microphone, a specific conferencing package – needed to complete all units of the online course. Do all prospective participants have these resources? How much responsibility should the institution take for making sure all the target groups have the necessary equipment and compatible systems? Does the institution have

a policy of standardizing the requirements, at least across a degree program, so that students do not need different, possibly incompatible, equipment and software for each online course? What measures are taken to reduce the financial burden of studying online, especially in countries such as Germany where, in addition to those of the Internet service provider, the telephone company charges by the minute?

2   *How computer-literate are the participants?* To participate actively and successfully, both students and teachers must be well versed in the use of the technology and software used in the course. The participants will either have this know-how already or must learn it fairly quickly and efficiently at the start of the course. Are the requirements made clear to students before they register in the seminar? How does the institution ensure that all subscribers to the course are competent enough and are provided with enough support to avoid the frustrations and failures associated with insufficient understanding of how the technology works?

3   *Who are the students in the online courses?* The virtual university is often seen as a quasi "natural" extension of open and distance education systems. Arising from the above questions on resources and computer literacy is the issue of selection. Many prospective distance students who would enroll in courses based on traditional media, and possibly a stand-alone computer, find it difficult or impossible to register as online students or to enroll in courses that are offered solely online because they do not own the necessary equipment and have inadequate or no access to a computer and the Internet (Hauff *et al.* 1999). Does this lead to systematic discrimination against specific target groups on the basis of social background, gender, or ethnic and cultural characteristics? Are these groups adequately represented among online students? What are the dropout and completion rates in online compared with other courses? Do students enroll in further virtual seminars once they have experienced one? How essential is participation in online courses for the completion of the degree, that is, must students take this specific seminar, or have they freely chosen an online seminar over a face-to-face course? What motivates students to choose online seminars over studying in the traditional distance mode? Are students more interested in the study mode and in working with the new media? Do they see online studying, with its possibilities of communicating with other students and with teachers, as a means to overcome the isolation of being a distance student?

Conclusion

We see a need for continued vigilance and action. To the extent that ICTs replace the traditional media, and access to advanced technologies becomes an essential prerequisite for studying in the virtual university, there is an increasing danger that women may be disproportionately disbarred from entering – and enjoying – the virtual learning environment. An institution that strives for gender equity must, in our opinion, be committed to presenting itself on the Internet/WWW in a nonsexist, gender-inclusive way, have an explicit policy regarding the design and content of Web sites, institute monitoring procedures with sanctions for offenses, and take measures to educate users in "netiquette."

Based on our research and experience, our conclusion is that the virtual university must not be left alone to develop "naturally," following techno-logical advances and software revolutions without regard to their social effects. As feminist researchers, we have a vested interest in ensuring the participation of women in the virtual university, and as evaluators of distance education, we wish to uncover factors that hinder this equal participation and measures that might be taken to redress gender imbalances.

References

Balka, E. and Smith, R. (eds) (2000) *Women, Work and Computerization: Charting a Course to the Future*. Dordrecht: Kluwer Academic.

Baumgartner, P. (1999) "10 Todsünden in der Medienevaluation Interaktiver Lehr- und Lernmedien," in K. Lehmann (ed.) *Studieren 2000. Alte Inhalte in neuen Medien?* Münster: Waxmann Verlag.

Belenky, M.F., Clinchy, B.M., Goldberger, N.R., and Tarule, J.M. (1986) *Women's Ways of Knowing: The Development of Self, Voice, and Mind*. New York: Basic Books.

Gilligan, C. (1982) *In a Different Voice: Psychological Theory and Women's Development*, Cambridge, MA: Harvard University Press.

Hansen, H. (2000) "Kongressbesprechung 'Women, Work and Computerization. Charting a Course to the Future.' Vancouver/Kanada vom 8.–11.6.2000". Unpublished paper, Trier: Universität Trier.

Hauff, M. (1999) "Multimedia: Perspektiven für Frauen – Perspektiven von Frauen," in M. Hauff, G. Kirkup, and C. von Prümmer (eds) *Frauen und neue Medien: Nutzung und Nutzen des Internets am Arbeitsplatz Hochschule und im Studium*. Hagen: FernUniversität.

Hauff, M., Kirkup, G., and von Prümmer, C. (eds) (1999) *Frauen und neue Medien: Nutzung und Nutzen des Internets am Arbeitsplatz Hochschule und im Studium*. Hagen: FernUniversität.

Herbst, I.M., Müller, H.J., and Voelker, S. (1994) *Mütter lernen anders! Eine Studie zur Weiterbildung für Familienfrauen durch Fernunterricht*. Wuppertal: Bergische Universität GHS.

Heron, M. (1997) *In My Own Skin: Dialogues with Women Students, Tutors and Counsellors. Researching Reality, Meaning, Change and Growth in the Open University*. Milton Keynes: Open University, Regional Academic Services.

Holst, S. (2000) "Evaluation of Collaborative Virtual Learning Environments: The State of the Art," in F. Scheuermann (ed.) *Campus 2000. Lernen in neuen Organisationsformen*. Münster: Waxmann Verlag.

Kirkup, G. (1996) "The Importance of Gender," in R. Mills and A. Tait (eds) *Supporting the Learner in Open and Distance Learning*. Cambridge: Pitman.

Kirkup, G. (1999) "The Potential of the Internet for Women's Education," in M. Hauff, G. Kirkup, and C. von Prümmer (eds) *Frauen und neue Medien: Nutzung und Nutzen des Internets am Arbeitsplatz Hochschule und im Studium*. Hagen: FernUniversität.

Kirkup, G. and von Prümmer, C. (1990) "Support and Connectedness: The Needs of Women Distance Education Students," *Journal of Distance Education*, 5, 2, 9–31.

Kirkup, G. and von Prümmer, C. (1997) "Distance Education for European Women. The Threats and Opportunities of New Educational Forms and Media," *European Journal of Women's Studies*, 4, 1, 39–62.

Lunneborg, P.W. (1994) *OU UK Women: Undoing Educational Obstacles*. New York: Cassell.

Mason, R. (2000) "The Pedagogy of Virtual Learning," in F. Scheuermann (ed.) *Campus 2000. Lernen in neuen Organisationsformen*. Münster: Waxmann Verlag.

Minkwitz, R. (2000) "Begrüßung und Eröffnung," in Geschäftsstelle Evaluation der Universitäten NRW (eds) *Reform von innen. Evaluation an NRW Hochschulen*. Münster: Waxmann Verlag.

Oakley, A. (1974) *The Sociology of Housework*. Bath: Martin Robertson.

Peters, O. and De Boer, W.F. (2000) "New Didactics for WWW-based Learning Environments: Examples of Good Practice at the University of Twente," in F. Scheuermann (ed.) *Campus 2000. Lernen in neuen Organisationsformen*. Münster: Waxmann Verlag.

Thompson, J. (1983) *Learning Liberation: Women's Response to Men's Education*. London: Croom Helm.

von Prümmer, C. (1997) *Frauen im Fernstudium. Bildungsaufstieg für Töchter aus Arbeiterfamilien*. Frankfurt/Main: Campus Verlag.

von Prümmer, C. (1998) "Evaluation of Media and Technology at the German FernUniversität," *Open Learning*, 13, 3, 59–65.

von Prümmer, C. (1999) "Nutzung und Nutzen des Internets für Frauen an der FernUniversität," in M. Hauff, G. Kirkup, and C. von Prümmer (eds) *Frauen und neue Medien: Nutzung und Nutzen des Internets am Arbeitsplatz Hochschule und im Studium*. Hagen: FernUniversität.

von Prümmer, C. (2000) *Women and Distance Education: Challenges and Opportunities*. London: Routledge.

von Prümmer, C. and Rossié, U. (1987) *Gender-Related Patterns in Students' Choice of Major Subject: Selected Research Findings*. Hagen: FernUniversität.

von Prümmer, C. and Rossié, U. (1989) *Value of Study Centers and Support Services: Selected Research Findings*. Hagen: FernUniversität.

von Prümmer, C. and Rossié, U. (1994) *Kommunikation im Fernstudium: Ausgewählte Ergebnisse einer Befragung im Wintersemester 1992/93*. Hagen: FernUniversität.

von Prümmer, C. and Rossié, U. (1996) *Ausstattung von Fernstudierenden mit Computern: Ergebnisse einer repräsentativen Befragung von ordentlichen Studierenden der FernUniversität im Studienjahr 1995/96*. Hagen: FernUniversität.

von Prümmer, C. and Rossié, U. (2000a) *Einschreibverhalten von Studentinnen und Studenten der FernUniversität in den 90er Jahren*. Hagen: FernUniversität.

von Prümmer, C. and Rossié, U. (2000b) *Verfügbarkeit und Nutzung von Computern und Informations- und Kommunikationstechnologien (IuK) im Fernstudium*. Hagen: FernUniversität.

Wetterling, J.M. and Moonen, J.C.M.M. (2000) "Supporting Telelearning in the University of Twente: The Idylle project," in K. Lehmann (ed.) *Studieren 2000: Alte Inhalte in neuen Medien?* Münster: Waxmann Verlag.

14 Using learning technologies: A synthesis of challenges and guidelines

Elizabeth J. Burge

If this chapter is the last you read, you know many details about the use of learning technologies. Use this synthesis to see the highlights, and compare them with your own thinking. If this chapter is your entry into the book, use it to gain directions or mental signposts for the detail in the other chapters.

Here I record the key challenges in using learning technologies and the major guidelines for thoughtful technological practice as represented by my coauthors. These are daunting tasks: How can anyone adequately represent the power of the images, the professional arguments, and the personal experiences described in the chapters? It feels as difficult as another representation task mentioned by Barbara Spronk: "No one set of issues, no one voice, can readily represent these divergent realities." Margaret Haughey explains in the first chapter how the value of this book lies in the authors' extensive and skilled experience of various learning technologies. We asked our colleagues to be reflective, especially focusing on the values that guide their work. We sought writing that included the professional-as-person as distinct from the more usual style of professional distance and prescription. It is not easy to include this kind of personal information for public analysis, as I can attest (Burge *et al.* 2000).

As I write this chapter, I sit surrounded by paper notes on a standard office chair ergonomically modified with old newspapers to improve the physical relationship of my body to the desk and keyboard. It is a cold November Sunday evening in a fogbound, quiet city in the middle of Sweden. Circling inside my head are vivid, sometimes unquiet, images and thoughts from the chapters: rural Fulbe women in Nigeria listening to radios that are perched on their calabashes; evaluators carefully justifying their methodologies to their clients; the primary schoolteacher whose house lights are turned off as she tries to read her course materials; the Sudanese woman whose son had changed the family computer password without telling her; faculty members in the Caribbean worrying about extra workloads; a learner whose precious savings are wasted on the cost of a bus trip that could not happen because the bus broke down; the differences between mango trees and orange trees; and a tutor forgoing a summer's day outdoors to stay in the office struggling to gain some control over the boundaries between professional and private identities.

I recall too the pragmatic Tanzanian who argues that the technologies she really needs are household technologies to help her finish the daily housework faster to gain more time for studying. While I desultorily think about a newer Web browser, colleagues elsewhere in the world worry about finding enough light bulbs for their tutorial areas. As I currently experience a relatively homogeneous and affluent Scandinavian society, other societies divide dramatically along the rich and poor "faultlines" (in Barbara Spronk) – the divisions between high and low levels of personal and societal resources. When I used the seamless and reliable services of distance education tele-communications networks, it was easy to forget that they had grown out of skillful policy development and committed partnerships. Reflecting on my own experience can limit my understandings and reduce my alertness to the nuances of collegial reflection.

Stepping back from the images and their underlying realities, I notice how they refer more to the human than to the technological aspects of learning and teaching. This should be no surprise if I consider my own experience in distance education, but this is not my focus here. This chapter is, I hope, just long enough to provide an alternate way of connecting with the reflections of 19 experienced and proficient colleagues. The conversational style is a deliberate effort to help this engagement, using some of O'Rourke's (2001) advice about how best to use print as an effective learning technology.

To prepare this chapter, I reread carefully each final manuscript to extract the challenges and guidelines implicitly or explicitly stated by each author. I used a broad definition of learning technologies: any tool, old or new, that is designed to extend a learner's capacity for effective action and that requires skill and certain strategies to use efficiently. So print, face-to-face structured discussions, audio- and videocassettes, radio programs, the Web, computer conferencing, and audioconferencing fit this definition. I developed many lists of extracts before I iteratively analyzed and distilled them. Individual authors are not specifically identified for every challenge or guideline mentioned below, and I hope all authors accept that the categories finally chosen in some way adequately represent their thinking and experience. Looking at all my notes and lists, I believe that if we could address all the challenges to some degree, we would make significant progress; and if we had the resources and stamina to follow just the three "really vital guidelines," a future book title might modify the words of the famous Schumacher book (1973) and become *Relevance is Beautiful: A Study of Learning Technologies as if Learners Mattered*. But now it is time to hear the authors again as they describe the challenges and guidelines for using learning technologies. I end with some questions for further thought.

Challenges in using learning technologies

Although I group the challenges into three categories of fairly obvious elements, such a tidy arrangement does not mirror the real-world chaos and complexities. The categories are the conditions that affect learners in the learning context; the teaching enterprise, including tutors and librarians; and the work of policy developers and evaluators. Other categories are less apparent, for example, the assumptions and habitual practices nested in people, the hyperbole surrounding the promise of technologies, ethical issues, and gender-related issues; these are woven into the three major categories.

Challenges for learners

Here I "walk the talk" and take a learner's view, using a vignette that reflects the intentions of an educational institution and of an adult learner.

A 42-year-old finally has gained entry to the first two courses toward an undergraduate degree in management. During the past year she obtained advice from the university (a typical one) about the right program to take if she was accepted as a degree student; generally, she heard useful ideas from the staff, even though they looked young and somewhat time-stressed.

Since leaving high school she has worked full time and studied part time at a polytechnic to gain the first set of qualifications for working in the travel industry (that was 14 years ago). Along the way she learned a lot about life and about running busy offices where speed, accuracy, and dependability are essential. She decided to take on this study program because she needs the qualifications to apply for a job promotion. She is reasonably well paid as the full-time manager of a company travel office. Her unpaid work includes managing a family (husband who manages a veterinary office, two children, and four pets), caring for an ailing father who lives 15 km away, and being president of the town's Rotary Club. Having observed her stress from too many overtime hours at work, the family are not keen to see her spend a lot of time on these new studies, but they agree to take on some extra household duties. She has paid the tuition fees from her own savings, and there is no taxation relief for adults like her who continue their education. Fast and easy access to the home telephone and computer for coursework depends on her being able to pry her 16-year-old son off the keyboard and her 11-year-old daughter off the telephone; or she can wait until the house is quiet – usually later at night and after the television news and sports programs have ended or the volume has been turned down. Surely something can be negotiated here, especially about keeping the house tidy, the meals prepared, and the clothes laundered. It will be impossible to go online at work to talk with classmates and surf the Internet. When the family car is used on some weekends to shuttle children to various events, she can catch a bus or hitch a ride to the big regional study center 80 km away for those face-to-face sessions.

At 10:00 p.m. on a Thursday the house has now settled into a peaceful place. With some anticipation she opens the first big package of course materials. Inside is a real mix of items: the course guide for topic structure and learning assessments, tutor's introductions, library information, and the core course content – all contained in print-based material with some audio- and videocassettes. There is a Web site to check soon: it has other study documents that she can print at her convenience. She knew before applying for admission to the university that online activity would be mandatory, but it looks as if there is more than she expected. There is also some research work using e-library resources, and she will have to visit the regional study center several times per course to undertake intensive study with colleagues, prepare for examinations, and obtain extra tutoring. The courses appear to have been designed carefully with a mix of attractive-looking materials to use; each course specifies its own online software.

Clearly the university assumes that learners can easily, often, and at convenient times and reasonable costs access an online computer and audio-conferencing facilities. (Frankly, the institution has good links to a series of study centers scattered around the country; it promotes its expertise; and it wishes to be seen as keeping up with the latest technologies and not getting beaten by the competition.) The course scheduling is tight because there is much content to be covered, and students are advised to maintain a certain pace so that they do not fall behind or become unduly stressed. (Covertly, the institution needs to get learners through and out to boost their publicity work and their course completion statistics in order to enhance their competitive reputation and be eligible for more government money.) All students need to learn how to use any of the technologies (print, audio, and online) fairly quickly; it is their problem – they knew this when enrolling. The basic course package should reach the learner's doorstep or the nearest study center for him or her to pick up well before the start of the course when everyone gathers to meet and attend orientation. The tuition costs are as market-relevant as the institution dares make them.

The course packages (one of which arrived much later than expected) reveal quite a number of management theories to be learned, but not as many practical topics and tasks as she would have liked (maybe some choices will be offered later in the course). The photograph of the tutor is obviously professional (seems friendly enough, but what's behind that smile?), and he sounds academically competent in his welcoming letter (but can I safely ask "dumb" questions and get helpful answers?). There is a written suggestion that she has to take responsibility for her learning (that's OK; I just deliver the assignments on time; after all, this university is the education expert, not me). A fast scan of the assignments reveals quite a number of them (so focus my energy on these: save time and maximize my grade levels). She then looks more closely: the textbook (thick) was published last year; extra booklets from the university (nice-looking) look helpful; and there are two videocassettes (like watching TV for a change) and four audiocassettes (good! I like listening, but I refuse to listen to those course radio broadcasts at 6:00 a.m. or 11:00 p.m. on weekends). The VCR still works, and a tape player is around the house somewhere; if it has disappeared, perhaps the local study center people or a friend will lend one, preferably a sturdy portable one to withstand hiking and jogging while she listens (multi-tasking is a constant fact of her life, even leisure life). She now scans the course Web site, which looks quite sophisticated and helpful, with links to a library help desk (been there in the local library) and some new, academic-looking, full-text databases (not seen these before!), and links to many Internet sites for further research (wow!). She wonders about technical help if she cannot easily use the software: it had better be available at night or on weekends when she has time to study and think. She then reads the tutor's written expectation that she will regularly "talk" to others in the class and avoid, if possible, going beyond the deadlines set for group work in the online conferencing system. She hopes to meet some study buddies – people who can help her discuss the management theories and share their experience; they may even be around when some companionable complaining about course workloads will make her feel better. Looking around the room now, she thinks about sitting at the computer every few days and realizes that a better office chair (even a proper ergonomic one) would help support her weary bones while she studies. But her son's piano lessons and daughter's judo lessons come first. Each course, it now appears, uses separate software, so she must learn fast for the second course. To save some time a higher-speed Internet connection and a faster printer would help, and maybe even a bigger table. ... Oh, oh, it's 11:00 p.m., time to get some sleep before the alarm clock jolts her into a new day.

The deep breath you may have imagined hearing is partly from excited anticipation and partly from apprehension about being a university learner; will everything work as well and as easily as she hopes?

Nesting in this vignette and in the chapters are the major learner-related challenges for using learning technologies. The challenges are extensive and interwoven. For the access and entry stages of a course, the needs are for adequate advice and career information; timely assistance; well-designed, multimedia course materials; easy and consistent access to, and use of, various technologies; development or assessment of information literacy and e-library skills; efficient use of personal time and energy; on-time delivery of course material; and course content that meets real-world learning needs. During the course, the challenges include: managing coursework loads; getting adequate support from people in paid work and unpaid work contexts; using flexibility in course schedules; being pragmatic about assignments and using learning technology; wishing to follow personal preferences in finding and processing information; keeping secure a sense of identity and self-confidence; figuring out who the others in the course are and who will be the most helpful; and gaining enough personal resources to sustain effective learning, for example, enough quality time, money, transport, and freedom from undue stressors.

Each challenge interacts in various ways with one or more applications of old or new learning technologies. When the interactions operate in too many negative ways – for example, infrastructure failures in transport, communication, or security and order procedures, or loss of personal power to make decisions – then the dynamics of the learning context may become problematic and create dissatisfaction and reduce the chances for the magic to happen.

The learner chosen for the vignette is a woman, and particular gender-related factors are in play, but this is not to say that male learners do not also experience many challenges in learning. We just need to be clear, as Edith Mhehe's student explained, that "mango trees and orange trees are different, although they are all fruit trees" and that some orchards get more money spent on their trees than do others (Sweetman 1998). In many orchards one variety of tree tends to receive disproportionately enhanced access to the available nutritional resources (but some "farmers" are unaware of this or dismiss it).

Challenges for educators

I now move to the people who directly help learners reach their learning goals: the tutor, the librarian, and advisors. The challenges here relate to personal philosophies, tacit and explicit values, representations of identity, and technology adoption issues.

Educators of any stripe bring their own "ideological and generational wrappings" (Cavanaugh, Ellerman, Oddson, and Young) into their work, so an immediate challenge is to discern what is inside the wrapping. Not every teacher will have the same enthusiasm for, or experience of, using computer technology as many of their younger students: it takes more than chrono-logical years to reveal generational differences in attitude and skill. Inside the wrapping may be unexamined ideas about teaching, habitual behaviors, workload stressors, significant achievements and reward-seeking behaviors, feelings of difference from the younger generation or from other cultures, and certain expectations about courteous students and sensitive administrators. A teacher may be wrapped in the belief that technologically mediated teaching still means that the core task is to transmit information rather than to help the student learn constructively, that is, no paradigm shift from instruction to learning is seen to be necessary (Barr and Tagg 1995). Another teacher may be privately extremely concerned about the impact of any technology on academic quality, but feel pressured to experiment with it, because the "early adopters" – the first to adopt new technologies (Moore 1991) – often attract the attention of administrators. As several authors point out, introduction of learning technologies is expected to raise legitimate fears from most of the teaching staff, both the more cautious "early majority" and "late majority" adopters of technology (Moore 1991). They detect within minutes any discreet coercion from government or private sectors; and within seconds they detect oversimplified claims about the benefits of any new technology. They think about "copyright and career development" (Christine Marrett and Claudia Harvey). The two majority groups try to predict the longer-term

impacts on workload and time available, and some quietly experiment with the new technologies to assess their real usefulness. They learn fast about technological "black holes" (Suzanne Sexty) that swallow institutional resources (e.g., updating Web pages); they know about the trade-offs presented by each technology application; and they may expect some institutional rewards for their extra efforts to be innovative. Experienced teachers will know what they wish to select from any technology to help create the conditions for the wonder and magic that characterize good learning. They will become impatient with "clunky" software (Cavanaugh, Ellerman, Oddson, and Young) and examine the extent to which the alleged democratizing features of computer conferencing, for example, will work. Examining gender-related aspects of any technology use may demand courage from educators who work in contexts where the norm or typical learner is uncritically construed as male. These educators need to maintain constant vigilance to hold the theoretical validity of their position. Such vigilance may steal time, drain energies, and entail challenging the unchallengeable, for example, the assumption that a virtual university can be left to develop "naturally" on the grounds that women now have greater access to computers (Christine von Prümmer and Ute Rossié).

The complex challenge of identity representation is about how an educator (or learner for that matter) uses the features of any technology to present and maintain one or more aspects of his or her many identities. This challenge goes far beyond the usual body-language aspects of communication strategies; it digs deeply into the need to embody and locate our sense of self and our perceptions of others' selves in particular contexts (note in the second paragraph my tendency to locate my identity as an editor). Identity refers to authenticity of self, how different social contexts influence our selection of an appropriate image of self (whether as a photograph, drawing, words, or avatar metaphor). Identity presents additional challenges of then articulating this identified self into the always changing and not always visual environments of technologically mediated learning. "But how do we represent and articulate [our identity] if our identities are always unfixed?" (Gill Kirkup).

Diminishing institutional resources, any "tension between on-campus and distance education systems" in the same institution (Marrett and Harvey), and the (often) increased quantity and pace of interactive communications are three related challenges. When teachers, librarians, and other staff assist visible clients on campus as well as invisible clients at a distance, it is no surprise that the campus people may get preference (Judith Kamau). When key colleagues, for example, librarians, are not institutionally valued enough as educators in their own right to be automatically embedded in all distance education design, information literacy skill development, and course delivery, then the problem is compounded: the skills of librarians are wasted and administrators can argue that because e-libraries are now so common, the intermediary functions of librarians as a "keystone species" in the learning environment are no longer justifiable (Nardi and O'Day 1999).

Policy-related challenges

The challenges contained in the interlinked policy development and evaluation categories may be less visible, but still deliver significant impact. Judith Roberts, Erin Keough, and Lucille Pacey point to the difficulties of negotiating policy quickly but collaboratively among all relevant stakeholders: conditions that can seem mutually exclusive. Policy developers must consider the challenges of how, when, and where technology infrastructures will be set up, maintained, and upgraded and then decide when to be flexible in interpretation and pragmatic in action without compromising core operational principles. Even to discover the levels of technology use among students can be a challenge: "We seem to need reminding that it is essential to conduct needs assessment surveys" (Kamau). Course designers or software developers can use high-end technology and then assume that learners enjoy the same. Course-related policies are then implemented, only to be melted down later in the heat of users' negative reactions. Another policy challenge is any assumption that the virtual university can develop naturally, because the definition of *naturally* carries its own connotations of who exercises decision-making power for purchasing and who has easy access to technologies. Fiscal and ethical challenges are evident when institutions enshrine in policy the discreet transfer of costs to students under the guise of experimentation with innovative technologies or with the assumption that everyone now has easy and inexpensive access to computers, printers, and the Internet. Mary Thorpe reminds us of the challenge to evaluators to carry out "learner profiling" – not only in demographics profiling, but also in usage conditions: "programs may fail not because our basic ideas were poor, but because learners could not make effective use of what we offered." Evaluators must be simultaneously client-responsive and professionally independent in making judgments without "drowning" in too much collected data.

Generally, the challenges identified by these authors are based less in how to use them for market advantage, or how learners ought to use externally imposed technologies, and more in how to make them relevant to the learners' contexts; how to fit them into the most appropriate mix of learning activities needed for learners to be "confident social actors and producers of knowledge" (Kirkup). The chapters show measured, critically questioning stances and immunity to any "seductive experience" characterized by the attention-getting and promise-making associated with claims for new software (Khaslavsky and Shedroff 1999: 46). The chapters also show many savvy guidelines.

Guidelines for using learning technologies

Certainly the most vital guidelines, those most often seen in my notes, seem to be relatively few in number: challenge and critique; be respectful; and be relevant.

The really vital guidelines

Challenge and critique

Use different perspectives to examine the same problem; interrogate beyond the surface level of a statement; question assumptions about ownership of technology and how it plays out in gender terms; and question the relevance of traditional models of teaching and the various mythologies of practice. Assess the extent to which the stability of a stated mandate for action has any relationship to changing circumstances; question the assumed educational benefits of adopting technology; and check who benefits and at what cost. Challenge educational provision that makes too many demands on a learner's own resources. Ask unpopular questions, and question the assumptions behind institutional and telecommunication network policies. At a minimum keep "an open and inquiring mind" (Charlotte Gunawardena).

Show respect

Show respect for the realities of learners' lives, for the strength and pervasiveness of the barriers faced by many learners and would-be learners, for the heroic efforts some make to stay in courses and gain access to technologies. Pay attention to adult learners' needs for time-and-effort efficiencies, for self-esteem and embodied identities, and their diversity of learning styles and learning-to-learn skill levels. Admit that psychological defense mechanisms powerfully strengthen resistance when learners are confronted by the imposition of difficult-to-use technologies. Respect the lasting power of older but equally design-demanding technologies such as print. Ignore with some peril the brain's need to construct knowledge actively and grapple with real-world problems. Know the different strengths and weaknesses of each technology as it affects the learner's capacity to think independently and learn proactively. Accept that all educators, as satellites in a learner's universe, need to earn their place. Finally, show respect for how technological change will always produce some disruptions of earlier technologies and some reinventions of others in new guises, as well as "generate new versions of old issues" (Thorpe).

Be relevant

Success happens at the interface between learner and learning technology, not in the intended design by the institution. Success refers first to the learner, second to the institution or provider partnership. Being relevant in course design and technology application means providing a mix of learning technologies that are relevant to different learning styles. It means online messaging, meetings, and broadcasts that synchronize with the learners' life rhythms: it means breaking learning work into manageable chunks of time and effort. Relevance to learning style preferences means using a variety of formats to represent the information to be studied. Use local community settings and personal networks to facilitate psychologically comfortable and easily accessible course discussions. Use equipment that is ergonomically appropriate for older as well as younger bodies; use learning activities that are cognitively appropriate for different age, gender, and cultural groups. Conduct evaluations that focus on what really happened vis-à-vis each technology in actual use. We might well take the now technologically unfashionable term *correspondence* and redefine it to mean a strong yet flexible match between learner and any learning technology.

After those vital three guidelines, could there be any more?

Nearly as vital guidelines

1 Attend to professional competence. Show the courage of personal convictions and common sense. Learn some history about adopting technology, as any new technology will generate "new versions of old issues" (Thorpe).
2 Get all the logistical infrastructures right, thus enhancing the chances of the learners' cognitive infrastructures to work well. Attention to detail for the former is a virtue; positive elements in the latter may lead to the "magic" of teaching.
3 Integrate everything: course materials, advisory services, methods of learning, strategies for tutoring, and models of evaluation.
4 Get savvy enough to be able to influence policy-makers with pragmatic arguments that go beyond the politically naïve "goals of social access and the common good" (Roberts, Keough, and Pacey).
5 Keep any learning technology as transparent as possible, and when learners complain of opaqueness, listen: the problem usually lies in the design, not the learner.
6 Trust learners: allowed to become partners in educational designs, they can deliver excellent ideas.
7 Take faculty reactions to workloads and the impact of technology seriously and be seen to do so.
8 Take the long view; it may appear to be the slower route, but it is the smarter one. The tortoise did beat the hare in that famous fable.

Questions for an ending

Below are the questions that would not go away during my work on this chapter.

1 Which elements in any well-designed learning environment could not be classed as a learning technology?

2   Which multidisciplinary theoretical frameworks are out there to help me think about learning environments in more sophisticated and creative ways? If I used ecological theories, for example, how far might they challenge my preconceptions?

3   What might I be doing in my use of any learning technology that acts to block or diminish a learner's identity, self-competence, and self-esteem?

4   What does it really mean to be an ethical user of any learning technology?

5   How might I best maintain a strategic balance between old and new, tried and true learning technologies in the face of intense sales talk and administrative passion for innovation?

6   If any technology has the potential for both amplifying current practice and even transforming it, what are the criteria for a transformation? And who might best help me critique and assess the amplifying processes?

It is time to stop. May all your learning technologies be transparent and your reflections about practice a little clearer as a result of using this book.

References

Barr, R.B. and Tagg, J. (1995) "From Teaching to Learning – A New Paradigm for Undergraduate Education," *Change*, 27, 6, 13–25.

Burge, E.J., Laroque, D., and Boak, C. (2000) "Baring Professional Souls: Reflections on Web Life," *Journal of Distance Education*, 15, 1, 81–98.

Khaslavsky, J. and Shedroff, N. (1999) "Understanding the Seductive Experience," *Communications of the ACM*, 42, 5, 45–49.

Moore, G.A. (1991) *Crossing the Chasm: Marketing and Selling Technology Products to Mainstream Customers*. New York: HarperBusiness.

Nardi, B.A. and O'Day, V.L. (1999) *Information Ecologies: Using Technology With Heart*. Cambridge, MA: MIT Press.

O'Rourke, J. (2001) "Print," in E.J Burge (ed.) *The Strategic Use of Learning Technologies, New Directions for Adult and Continuing Education No. 88.* San Francisco, CA: Jossey-Bass.

Schumacher, E. (1973) *Small is Beautiful: A Study of Economics as if People Mattered*. London: Abacus.

Sweetman, C. (ed.) (1998) *Gender and Technology*. Oxford: Oxfam.

Index

access, and benefits of distance-mode
option 41; gender aspects 16, 21–3,
99–100, 137–9; and issue of timing 98;
and learner profiling 126–7; to cassette
players 54; to e-mail 15; to
educational experience 79–80; to
human/physical resources 44; to ICTs
138–9; to information 79; to the
Internet 16, 20, 44–5, 140; to library
Web-sites 85–6; to proposed media 53;
to technology 19–20, 22–3, 62–3, 93,
99–100, 140–1; to telecommunications
35, *see also* barriers to access
Association for Learning Technology
125
Athabasca University (AU) (Alberta,
Canada), described 61–3
audiocassettes 50, 52, 54, 72
audioconferencing 39, 40, 42, 44, 146

barriers to access 56; and benefits of
evaluation 131; cultural expectations
104–6; electricity/telephones 19–20;
financial resources 106–7; language
98–9; literacy 19; and marginalized
groups 16; overcoming 107–10; postal
delays 50; poverty 16–17; procedural/
attitudinal 49; time constraints 103–4;
transport 15, *see also* access
Botswana College of Distance and Open
Learning (BOCODOL) 49

Cambrian College (Canada) 28
Canadian Network for Advanced
Research in Industry and Education
Inc. (CANARIE) 32, 33
Canadian Radio-Television and
Telecommunications Commission
(CRTC) 34, 35

Caribbean Community (CARICOM)
39
CD-ROMs 66, 128
Commonwealth of Learning
5–6
community learning centers 22–3
computer technology, access to 15;
appeal of 67; caution concerning
67–8; challenges of 66; cost/
availability of 62–3; democratizing
aspects 66–7; effect on hierarchical
structures 62; effect of 63–4; impact
on teachers 62, 63–5, 66–7, 68;
ownership of 127; political/economic
assumptions 68; and problems of
adoption 64, 65; promise/experience
gap 62; recommendations concerning
adoption of 68–70; supposed
neutrality of 64–5; and teaching
objectives 63, *see also* online learning
computer-mediated communication
(CMC) 118, 128, 129, 130
computer-mediated teaching 74–5; and
question of embodiment 77–80;
situation 75; and student identity
75–6; and teacher authenticity 73,
76–7
Confederation College (Canada)
28
Connecting Canadians policy 27
Contact North/Contact Nord (CN/CN)
27–9; consultation 33–4; mandate 32;
policy areas 30–1; resources 33;
technology 34–5
Council of Atlantic University
Librarians/Conseil des
Directeurs(trices) de Bibliothèque des
Universités de l'Atlantique (CAUL)
84